Bread of Tears
דמעות של לחם

Based on
Psalms 80: 5

Lige Jeter

Bread of Tears

Copyright © 2000, 2015, Lige Jeter

All rights reserved as permitted under the United States of America Copyright act.

Printed in the United States of America

ISBN- 13: 978-0692364031
10: 069236403X

All Scripture quotations selected are from the *New King James Version*. Copyright 1997, 1980, 1982, by Thomas Nelson, Inc. Used by permission. Verse numbers omitted where quoted.

Reference quotations taken from *The Legal Alert,* Christian Law Association by David C. Gibbs Jr., non-copyrighted material, April 2000. Used by permission

Reference quotations taken from The *World Almanac and Book of Facts 2004,* Copyright 2004, World Almanac Education Group. Used by permission

Reference statistics quotations from *Barna research Group*, Ltd., Ventura, California. Copyright 1995-2003. Used by permission

Suggested Additional Resources:

Dr. Hertz, J. H., *Pentateuch & Haftorahs,* The Sonico Press, Second Edition, 5756-1996, (Jewish). This Hebrew-English edition contains the five books of Moses. It provides the reader with a spiritual and ethical teaching of the Torah. It contains the full Hebrew text, with line-by-line English translation including commentary.

Wiley H. Orton, *Introduction to Christian Theology,* Beacon Hill Press, Ninth Printing, 1959, (Nazarene). The doctrinal emphasis is Arminian and Wesleyan. The essential purpose is to provide a text as an introductory course in basic Theology, text friendly for the general use of the laity of the church.

Purkiser, W. T., PhD, *Exploring our Christian Faith,* Beacon Hill Press, First Printing, 1960, (Nazarene). This volume introduces evangelical Wesleyan Christianity described as part of the holiness movement. The scope of the book is primarily to the history of doctrine, to comparative religions, and the ethics and practices of the Christian life.

Purkiser, W. T., PhD, *Exploring the Old Testament,* Beacon Hill Press, Third Printing, 1957, (Nazarene). This was, written to serve as a textbook, for basis college entry-level study of the Old Testament.

Earle, Ralph, Th.D., *Exploring the New Testament,* Beacon Hill Press, Second Printing, 1956, (Nazarene). This book was prepared as a textbook for required studies in New Testament survey for the beginning student in college.

ACKNOWLEDGMENTS

To God is the glory forever for His inspiration and divine guidance in writing this book. The debt to Him, whom I owe everything, is more than one can ever repay. Without His help, this book would have been impossible.

I am indebted to all my friends who down through the years have touched my life in many ways and have made a profound difference in my Christian walk. To them I owe an enormous gratitude of thanks.

To my family whom God has given me, are my richest blessings in life. To them, I dedicate this book.

CONTENTS

FORWARD	8

PART I
Holiness a Way of Life
God's Standard for Living

INTRODUCTION	14
CHAPTER 1	17

Opinions Matter
Proceed with Caution

CHAPTER 2	22

God in All Creation
Elohim and Adonay

CHAPTER 3	32

Beginning of Life
The First Family

CHAPTER 4	41

Consequence of Sin
Sowing and Reaping

CHAPTER 5	50

Law and Grace
Past vs. Present

CHAPTER 6	61

Holiness God's Command
Rags to Riches

CHAPTER 7   70
God's Divine Blueprint
Road to Success

CHAPTER 8   77
Highway to Heaven
No u Turn

CHAPTER 9   84
Our Journey Begins
Pack Your Bags

CHAPTER 10   96
Filled With His Spirit
Full vs Empty

CHAPTER 11   110
Our Final Destination
Finally Home

BONUS CHAPTER
CHAPTER 12   116
Redemption
Debt Paid

DEFINITIONS   133
LESSON OUTLINE   138
SCRIPTURE REFERENCE   158

PART II   160
A Nation in Turmoil
9-1-1

FOREWORD
Part I

In April 2000, established upon time-honored biblical truth, I began writing *Holiness A Way of Life,* with the explicit purpose to awaken our nation to its current spiritual state of affairs. For more than two decades, I have been genuinely concerned about what is happening across America. Without being judgmental, given the laissez-faire direction many have chosen drifting away from moral living, inspired this book.

A large number of those professing a relationship with Christ upon leaving the church service conduct their lives on par with those in the world who do not profess anything. It is a sad day in Christendom when it becomes difficult to distinguish the churched group by their behavior from the un-churched. At present, statistics taken by reputable organizations such as the Barna group supports this finding.

There are many social activities today currently accepted by society as the norm once held taboo by the church. Some, attending church, professing being Christian perform many of these same activities in the same manner. These deeds include but are not limited to social drinking, smoking, coarse jokes, foul language, drugs, pornography, and other sensual activity, etc...

One outstanding undeniable paradigm is the divorce rate in the church community that matches with the secular world. If the unsaved are to catch a glimpse of Christ we must separate ourselves from the world we have come to love, and come back to holy living.

While holiness identifies a way of life for the church, individual holiness without doubt is one of the most difficult concepts taught in the Bible. Principally, because of its peculiarity or characteristics ascribed to one's personal conduct holding them accountable to God and the assembly at large.

As God's Word confirms, it becomes one's apparent responsibility to live according to God's plan. For that reason, without exception, they are predominantly accountable for their activities while here upon earth as instructed

> *Because it is written, Be holy, for I am holy. The Father who without partiality judges accordingly to each one's work, conduct yourselves throughout the time of your stay here in fear* (1 Peter 1: 13 – 17 text not printed in its entirety).

Peter encourages the Jewish believers in Christ who are struggling to conduct themselves boldly to live above reproach. He instructs them to be obedient and not to conform to their former lusts but to be holy in all their conduct, *Be holy, for I am holy.* This is not a request or option but a command; this is why holiness is so important. This is Good advice for anyone!

Part II

We are not the first nation to stray from its founding principles. A nation's decline usually occurs when they began to drift from the values that made them strong. The pages of history are full of literary works depicting such events. No doubt without exception they too failed to heed the warning signs leading to their downfall.

As a powerful warning against such activity, I have been encouraged to write *A Nation in Turmoil*. Moses reiterates God's Word commanding the children of Israel not to remove or alter their heritage.

> *You shall not remove your neighbor's landmark, which the men of old have set, in your inheritance which you will inherit in the land that the Lord your God is giving you to possess. Cursed is the one who moves his neighbor's landmark (*Deuteronomy 19: 14, 27: 17).

Landmarks in the Old Testament were sacred to the Jewish race. It literally meant the difference between a family's survival or demise. One's existence depended largely upon whether or not their property was encroached' upon by a greedy neighbor. In moving, another's landmarks increased his property to gain more wealth.

The removal of one's boundary was a serious crime, understood in *you shall not remove,* placing them under the penalty of a curse. The curse here alludes to the judgment and wrath of God upon the guilty party.

Solomon reaffirms God's Word as a wise reminder to His people and all future generations. *Do not remove the ancient landmarks which your fathers have set (*Proverbs 22: 28). We can extract from this several parallel truths.

For the church, we are to guard against bringing in new doctrines, baseless teachings, or false fabrications as we are seeing today. The church should avoid any form of pagan or secularism that undermines genuine worship and compromises moral living taught in holy writings. Moreover, these same principles and safeguards are applicable to society as well.

As a nation for some time, we have been pulling up our ancient landmarks. We are replacing the Godly with the ungodly. Our nation, as a people is in serious trouble unless we turn around and come back to the sound moral principles upon once founded. For that reason, we are to hold these landmarks as sacred.

My only request is that you read this book keeping in mind the truth applied to the nation, are for you as well. No one is an island unto himself or herself.

About the Author

Church Affiliation:
Church of the Nazarene
Scholastics Endeavors:
Master-of-Science - 1984, Nova University
Administration and Supervision
Bachelor-of-Divinity - 1971, Luther Rice Seminary
Pastoral Ministry
Bachelor-of-Science - 1970, Trevecca Nazarene University
Elementary Education
Military Service: *(twelve years active and reserve)*
United States Air Force

United States Navy
United States Navy Reserve (Seabees)
Chaplain Civil Air Patrol, Lt. Col. (Auxiliary United States Air Force)
Professional Experience:
    In my earlier years in the ministry, I served as senior pastor in the church, pasturing two churches. I spent the last twenty-three years in Corporate America with a major telecommunications company before retiring. It is widely believed that, "Adversity is a great teacher." To this I say, "A hearty Amen."

    The combined religious training I received and my secular opportunities have given support and sustenance in keeping a balance in the pursuit of truth. Without seeming brash one has kept my head out of the clouds and the other my feet on solid ground.

    I believe the search for balance in this life and the life to come is the desire of us all. The primary objective is to enlighten the convert to the importance of holiness and to seek its fullness. In counterpart, to educate the reader concerning salvation, and warning about God's punishment to those who do not know Him?

About the Bible

    The Holy Bible is the only compilation of writings that spans a period of over fifteen hundred years, with approximately forty different writers with various vocations such as Prophets, Poets, Shepherds, Scholars, Priests, Tax collectors, and Fishermen. The Bible's written in different languages, Hebrew, Aramaic, and Greek. Never have there ever been any other book translated into as many languages, or sold as many copies worldwide.

    From Genesis to Revelations appointed by God who inspired the writers. Paul in his letter to Timothy confirms this truth. *All Scripture is given by inspiration of God, and profitable for doctrine, for reproof, for correction, for instructions in righteousness (*2 Timothy 3: 16). It has God's signature all over it, and no other book in the world can make this claim. The Bible conveys one consistent message and that is Jesus Christ.

The fact that the Bible has survived for centuries should be all the proof that a person needs to believe its sacred truths. History has proven this and Isaiah alludes to the passing of time in relationship to the endurance of the Word of God. *The grass withers, the flower fades, but the word of our God stands forever* (Isaiah 40: 8). Only God has the power to preserve His Word by whatever means He chooses without man's approval.

Peter reiterates the words of Isaiah when writing to the church during the midst of persecution, encouraging them to trust in the gospel of salvation entrusted to them. He proclaims to the church that God's enduring word will outlive them.

> *All flesh is as grass, And all the glory of man as the flower of the grass. The grass withers, And its flower falls away, But the word of the LORD endures forever. Now this is the word which by the gospel was preached to you* (1 Peter 1: 24 – 25).

The most important witness, Jesus the Alpha and Omega, confirms to His disciples and the rest of the world the continued existence of His Word. *Heaven and earth will pass away, but My words will by no means pass away* (Matthew 24: 35).

The Bible is the inspired inerrant infallible Word of God in every aspect, and can be fully trusted in all of its content and teachings of divine truth. It contains Jehovah's revelation of Himself, giving man an insight into his creation, where he is bound, and his pathway on how to get there.

The Bible communicates God's holiness and conveys man's responsibility in relationship to his Creator. The sixty-six books articulate God's interaction with humanity pertaining to man's redemption in both this present world and the world to come. No other book or books can make this claim; therefore, man is without excuse of wrongdoing.

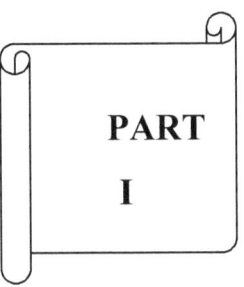

PART I

HOLINESS A WAY OF LIFE

God's Standard for Living

Leviticus 11: 44, I Peter 1: 16

INTRODUCTION

WHAT IF, you were God! Without equal in power, infinite in knowledge, transcendent in time, past, present, and future, what kind of a universe would you create. What life form would you bring into existence to inhabit your world, assuming you would fashion human beings as now exist?

It is plausibly that you would fashion them to possess some of your qualities as being immortal, gifted with freedom of choice, and given moral character reflecting those of their Creator; undoubtedly, you would want them to have fellowship with you.

How would you expect them to live and conduct themselves in society? What instructions or set of laws would you give your new creation to promote harmony and a peaceful co-existence? Would they be free to execute upon earth anything they please without regard to their neighbor, or their Creator?

These are tough uncompromising questions without easy answers, maybe God though about those same things.

One thing's for certain, God has an achievable purpose for our lives which is an "identifiable and obtainable" moral standard of living for all humankind. That standard is holiness!

The Bible is unmistakably clear upon the subject, and teaches that we are to live consecrated lives. What's more, it clearly states that, without holiness, no one will see the Lord.

> *Speak to all the congregation of the children of Israel, and say to them; "You shall be holy, for I the Lord your God am holy"* (Leviticus 19: 2). *Pursue peace with all people, and holiness, without which no one will see the Lord* (Hebrews 12: 14).

Holiness without a doubt is the righteous focal point found in both the Old and New Testament. Some may prefer to believe otherwise does not change nor nullify this truth.

Many in our populace today have vacated the truth, and have accepted the social values placed upon them by society in exchange for the Word of God. This comes from the fact that many in the human race now have a distorted sense of belief on how humanity is to live morally.

Holy living is not one single denomination's belief but is widely accepted by a number of churches across America. It was God's intent in the beginning with Adam and it is God's will today. Sad but a large number no longer believe in the truth of the Bible.

In Hermeneutics (the systematic approach of interpreting the Bible) in Seminary, we were taught to go back to the law of first mention when interpreting the Bible. Some well-meaning Christians often take an isolated passage of Scripture and build a doctrine of truth for themself that fits their life style.

The problem when doing this is the alleged truth often contradicts other apparent Scriptures. In Biblical study, this is a cardinal sin.

To avoid the risk of conjecture it is essential we start with the book of Genesis. Here we have our first insight into man's original sinless nature reflecting holiness and follow what transpires to understand our own spiritual dilemma.

To understand the problem we need to start with how it all initially began to comprehend the meaning of holiness, sometimes referred to as perfect love, entire sanctification, or Christian perfection.

In the pursuit of truth, I will endeavor to answer according to the Word of God the following seven questions that have plagued humanity for centuries.

1. **Is God the Divine Creator of all that exists and apart from Him nothing exists?**
2. **Is humankind eternally lost in his present condition?**
3. **Can man be, saved, from his sinful state?**
4. **Is Jesus Christ the only one who can forgive sin and set one free from sin?**
5. **Is holiness relevant as a pre-condition to seeing God?**
6. **Is holiness obtainable in the 21st century?**
7. **Is there a final judgment where all humankind will receive their eternal reward that will determine their final abode of heaven or hell?**

My prayer, whether you are in a study group or reading alone, that you will be open to the Holy Spirit and the truth revealed in His Word. It is not my purpose to condemn anyone, only to show plainly in Christian love God's Word to change lives

CHAPTER I

Opinions Matter

Proceed with Caution

Try the Spirits:
Beloved, do not believe every spirit, but test the spirits, whether they are of God; because many false prophets have gone out into the world (1 John 4: 1).

This chapter's objective is to encourage the reader to examine ones belief system especially with so much confusion in churches today.

Take some advice; before you begin this book or any other religious book, do not be eager to believe every teacher or preacher because of his or her credentials or claim to be of God.

I say this cautiously because John taught that many pretend to teach and preach under the influence of the Holy Spirit. He instructs us to try those, and put them to the test, according to the Word of God. The fact that *many false prophets have gone out into the world* spells apprehension in discerning the genuine from the false, or a mixture of truth and assumption.

The foundation that you build your life upon will determine how you live. What one believes about God's Word or disbelieves have caused great anguish to God's people whether intentional or unintentional depending upon your point of view.

There are numerous disagreements on biblical topics debated in churches across America. Each based upon how one interprets certain selected Scripture.

It is important, as in any teachings, always ask the Holy Spirit to give you discernment pertaining to God's truth in spiritual affairs over men's opinion. Short of judgment, the following well-debated famous example illustrates this very well and leaves the reader with a choice to make which holds the greater truth for them.

Age-old Debate

In Theological circles, there remains the age-old argument of the doctrinal teaching of John Calvin (1509 – 1564), vs. Jacob Arminius (1560 – 1609). Calvin, greatly influenced by Augustine's doctrine of predestination, and later taught as unconditional election. Arminius set out to disprove Calvin by teaching that election was conditional based upon personal faith; therefore, the possibility of falling from grace existed.

Divisions like these within the body of Christ continue to cause confusion and spiritual anguish among believers as it pertains to their conscience. Am I saved or am I lost (or backslidden) is the impasse here?

There will always be debate among churches about whether or not you can live the Spirit filled life and fulfill our role before God as part of the "Holy Royal Priesthood." These issues should never become the main focal point, neither become paramount to the church's teaching; nor can entirely be dismissed either. What you believe will influence your spiritual consciousness in understanding and dealing with sacred truths.

While I was attending Luther Rice Seminary a wise professor (Dr. Smith) expounding upon this very subject, offered his students some good advice. He believed that the teachings of Calvin and Arminius took their doctrine too far.

He taught that it was extreme and judgmental to conclude that a person can never be lost after coming to Christ regardless of their lifestyle or that a person has actually turned their back upon God and be lost after believing.

> **Footnote**: Luther Rice Seminary is a private non-denominational Seminary that I attended. The school founded in 1962, and the first classes met on September 11. All faculty members were Southern Baptist pastors who served initially without pay.
>
> Upon enrollment, I had to state my doctrinal beliefs prior to acceptance. The major difference was I believed the teaching of Wesleyan-Arminian over the teaching of

Calvin concerning man's free will after coming to Christ. My opposing position never became an issue, which is a testimony to their fairness and the pursuit of academic excellence in pursuit of truth.

I am convinced the truth lies somewhere between the two dogmas. The Holy Spirit is the only one capable of knowing the truth concerning all the facts involving the person or sin. The truth of God's acceptance or rejection of one's actions belongs to Him and Him alone.

There is Only One Judge

The Holy Spirit is the only one who is capable of doing this in the life of the believer. Jesus spoke of this in His gospel. One would be wise to trust the Holy Spirit rather than man's opinion in these matters and here is the reason why.

> *.... when He has come, He will convict the world of sin, and of righteousness, and of judgment. However, when He, the Spirit of truth, has come, He will guide you into all truth; for He will not speak on His own authority, but whatever He hears He will speak; and He will tell you things to come* (John 16: 8, 13).

When differences of belief collide over right and wrong and you cannot decide or discern the obvious on which is correct then you must rely upon a higher wiser power other than your own understanding; *the Holy Spirit will guide you into all truth.*

The Apostle Paul lived by these principles, and did not deem that he needed to enter into a debate over his innocence or guilt before men. This is not to imply that Paul did not give, or receive wise counsel from his peers, as should we, if directed by the Holy Spirit.

He was content to leave those things to God, and that God would make known in his favor and not he himself. Try God's counseling first, this is sound advice for everyone!

> *Moreover it is required in stewards that one be found faithful. But with me it is a very small thing that I should be judged by you or by a human court.*

> *In fact, I do not even judge myself. For I know nothing against myself, yet I am not justified by this; but He who judges me is the Lord* (1 Corinthians 4: 2 – 4).

The term *that one be found faithful* suggests the enquiry on how can one be found faithful. The word "faithful" implies that of a marriage between a man and a woman devoted to each other. God often used marriage in describing His relationship to Israel.

He used the illustration to define their faithfulness and to expose their unfaithfulness to him similar to that between a husband and spouse. The purpose of marriage is to preserve and sanctify that which God has ordained.

Paul understood that if there were anything wrong between him and God, pertaining to him being unfaithful, he would be the first to know about it; therefore, did not rely upon the judgment of man. He recognized that God's judgment is impartial and flawless. He was more than confident that God would make it known to him, and he could trust God's wisdom in matters of sin over others opinion including his own.

In whom are you putting your trust? Is it man, and you allow him to be your judge in questions pertaining to the heart, or God who says that His grace is sufficient? In 1 Samuel, we have a window of truth where true judgment takes place between man and God. In addition, in Matthew, Jesus warns us about judging others.

> *For the Lord does not see as man sees; for man looks at the outward appearance, but the Lord looks at the heart* (1 Samuel 16: 7b). *Judge not, that you be not judged. For with what judgment you judge, you will be judged; and with the measure you use, it will be measured back to you* (Matthew 7: 1 – 2).

In spiritual terms, *the heart* depicts the moral wholeness or center of our universe as it relates to us as a created being. One's outward appearance seeking recognition or approval can be deceptive without being genuine in appearance or accomplishments. For that reason, man is incapable of judgment because he cannot judge the true motive; therefore, we are not to judge.

Only the Creator is capable of knowing our motives in relationship to Him. However, caution involving our Christian witness illustrated by our outward conduct should remain a priority, and does not give one liberty to sin recognized by committing wrongful behavior.

We are One Body Sharing Responsibility

The body of Christ should never take the spiritual wellbeing of fellow believers lightly. Perhaps now more than ever, churches share a responsibility toward the followers of Christ.

Every believer should daily encourage each other in the Lord as instructed to ... *exhort one another daily, while it is called 'today,' lest any of you be hardened through the deceitfulness of sin* (Hebrews 3: 13).

We can honestly say that dialogue is healthy in reaching a mutual understanding. Providing the participants are open minded without being prejudice, or being inconsiderate about biblical truths. It is when we are open to the truth, that we find it.

Whether you follow the teaching of Calvin or Arminius, will have a direct correlation on how you live your Christian life. I encourage you not to become so entrenched that you ignore the Holy Spirit and what He is telling you.

CHAPTER 2

God in all Creation

Elohim and Adonay

In the Beginning:
In the beginning, God created the heavens and the earth (Genesis 1: 1).

The First verse in the Old Testament is without doubt one of the most essential verses found in the Bible. When labelled an allegory as some have, there would be little need for the rest of the Old or New Testament. You choose to ignore this verse you may as well ignore the rest of the sacred book. Genesis chapters one through three are the most important chapters in God's Holy Word.

Without it, humankind would wander all his days in darkness, never knowing where he came from, nor could believe where he was bound for, or how to get there. The creation chapters of Genesis without faith defy all of man's wisdom and leaves humanity with questions without logical answers.

For this reason, man in his own genius has proffered his own theory of creation, apart from God. Men like Charles Darwin offered "evolution" to explain our universe rather than accept the Genesis account. Evolution is a human substitute solution explaining creation lacking adequate proof to substantiate its claims.

Creation is too complex for humankind to understand or explain adequately, let alone define in unproven scientific evolutionary terms. Job learned a painful lesson of humility concerning the Omnipotence of God that science could benefit from. More in detail on Job later

Let us first examine evolution as man's attempt to explain creation and see the impact it has on society. In addition, we will look at how it has influenced the church, tainting the belief of biblical creation among those who attend church regularly. It is of little surprise that many have come to believe there is no God; and have invented many so-called truths about man's spirituality that leaves him without hope beyond this life.

Evolution

The word evolution comes from the Latin *evolvere* indicating to change gradually. One of the leading well-known proponents of evolution known as the "Father of evolution" was Charles Darwin (1809 – 1882). It is impossible to cover his life in depth, therefore, for our purposes will only deal with those pieces illustrating the digression in his life that led him to become an agnostic.

Darwin is well known and celebrated for his work, *The Origin of Species*. His works paved the way for a prevailing acceptance of "evolution by natural selection," which advocates or teaches change occurs among the species by natural selection without divine involvement or intervention.

I believe it is important to look at the life of Darwin to see the impact his devotion to the subject of evolution causing him to denounce his belief in God. His chosen path of disbelief should serve as a warning to all of us.

Charles Darwin was born on February 12, 1809 in Shrewsbury, Shropshire, England and died on April 19, 1882 in Down House, Downe, Kent, England. Darwin's church affiliation, an Anglican, baptized in the Church of England and reared under Unitarian influence by his mother.

He attended the University of Edinburgh and dropped out of medical school after two years. He studied three years at Christ's College Cambridge where he encountered theology.

For whatever reason Darwin's faith began to crumble when he began to doubt the story of creation as taught in Genesis. He began to accept theories of men like Charles Lyell, who believed that everything in nature came about by accident rather than by divine means. The more Darwin embraced teachings of men like 'Lyell' the more he began to question the Bible.

In his writings at age forty, Darwin gave up on Christianity and in 1880; he wrote that he no longer believed in the Bible as a divine revelation of God, or in the Son of God. This is a sad commentary, in the life of one so brilliant, who had much to offer the world.

One might ask how someone with his background could ever come to deny God. To this, we may never find a suitable answer. The truth is when a person begins to question God's Word can lead them to embrace a life of doubt and later denial, and in the end, that person will be eternally lost.

The unsolved mystery that we may never know, did Darwin become a Christian between 1880 and his death in 1882, when he professed he no longer believe the Bible or in Jesus Christ?

Lady Hope, who told the only story of his conversion, claimed she visited Darwin who was ill at his Down House in 1881, found him reading the book of Hebrews. She later quoted Darwin, asking her back to speak about Jesus.

His family denied the story as this ever occurring. A limited historical/biographical account on Charles Darwin and Lady Hope can be located using *Wikipedia*, the online free encyclopedia.

Evolutionary Influence

Darwin's theory of Natural Evolution, denies the existence of a Creator God. Evolution no longer taught in our schools as a theory, but as a scientific fact for over a quarter century. According to a recent Gallup poll posted in 2009, the influence of the theory of evolution and its impact upon students have no doubt had an effect on their belief about God as these statistics show.

Those who believe in evolution are:

74 percent of post graduate students.
53 percent of college graduate students.
41 percent of students with some college,
21 percent of high school students.

Those students who have no opinion:

16 percent post graduates.
26 percent college graduates.
30 percent some college, and
52 percent high school students.

What is interesting is the correlation in the poll of percentages related to the degree of education.

At the high school level, fifty-two percent had no opinion while twenty-one percent believed in evolution.

At the post-graduate level, seventy-four percent believed in evolution and only sixteen percent had no opinion.

It appears the more education one has the easier it becomes to believe in evolution. The reverse is true when compared to those with a lesser education.

This is a clear warning of the power of intellectual manipulation. Those who seek a higher education should beware of its influence and not be caught off guard.

How do Americans rate overall? In 2005 according to the Gallup poll twenty-nine percent of Americans believed in evolution compared to thirty-nine percent in 2009. This is a significant gain in four years.

According to the polls, there is no denying that evolution has made a huge impact even among churchgoers. Gallup reported in 2009, that twenty-four percent of those who attend church weekly believe in evolution. Reportable that number grows to fifty-five percent among those who seldom or never attend church. The reflection of church attendance is clear.

What we are seeing is an attack on creation as taught in the book of Genesis to discredit the Bible and those who believe in God. It is therefore my opinion if we doubt creation as taught in God's Word we will begin to question other specific truths relating to heaven or hell; or the need for salvation; or the need for holy living. We are seeing evidence this is already happening.

Creation

As Solomon wrote, *there is nothing new under the sun* (Ecclesiastes 1: 9b). This Scripture' been expressed in various ways by numerous biblical scholars expressing similar measures of interpretation of its meaning. In unity with them, I will be brief and only point out those topics that pertain to this portion of text explaining creation as it relates to God as Creator and His involvement after creation.

The Hebrew word for "Book of Creation" is *Sefer Maaseh Bereshith.* We recognize it best by its Greek name *Genesis* meaning origin. The book is unique in the fact that it declares God as the Creator apart from all things that exists. It gives details to the origin of man, and his relationship to God, tying all humankind together from Adam.

These two indispensable thoughts in Jewish teaching are important to our study. They express how we see God in nature, and His relations with humanity. This is expressed by His loving mercy shown by His grace and impartial justice revealed in His righteousness.

The Pentateuch (Greek for the five books of Moses) is more than a code of civil and religious laws. It is the Torah the Divine Teachings of Israel with its message to humankind. The first eleven chapters, gives us an account of creation of the world and the beginning of life and society. It declares it the work of one almighty and beneficent God.

These viewpoints expressed in two Hebraic words, *Elohim* (justice) *and Adonay* (mercy). These Hebrew names given to God convey His exact nature found in Scripture. This is crucial in understanding the correct meaning as it applies to the Creator.

For God (*Adonay*) to create the world by mercy alone without lawfulness, sin would prosper without cure. To create the same world by justice alone (*Elohim*) without mercy, then the world would cease to exist, as we know it. Both *Adonay* and *Elohim* together describe His justness and mercifulness.

Examples of both of these were in the saving of Noah and his family before the flood. God's impartial justice condemned the world of sin destroying the wicked, while His grace and mercy to the righteous shut the door to the ark before the flood.

Additionally, in Jewish discernment certain passages portray parallel truths about God. These truths are very important in understanding His absolute perfection! *Then God said,* (Genesis 1: 3) carries the same concept as *God willed,* meaning all of creation was intentional as planned and could not have happened by chance since Scriptures tells us; *By the word of the Lord the heavens were made* (Psalms 33: 6a). *All things were made through Him, and without Him nothing was made that was made* (John 1: 3).

The words, *that it was good* (Genesis 1: 4) acknowledge the will of God fulfilled in His creation. This phrase was, repeated five additional times in the creation story. Likewise when God said; *it was very good* (Genesis 1: 31) suggesting in itself that all He created was according to His will. He was pleased with every part in existence, and was satisfied that nothing was lacking in the whole of His creation. These expressions of satisfaction are very important as an insight into God's personal pleasure conveyed during creation.

In the original Hebrew, the Torah never divided itself into chapters and verses as we have today. Perhaps this is why some believe there are two accounts of creation. The first account found in chapter one and the second account in chapter two. In effect, they are the same expressed somewhat differently for different purposes.

In Genesis 2: 1 – 3, belongs in chapter one. This makes sense when you apply this as a continuance of creative days. Therefore, it is logical the second chapter would begin with the following narrative. *This is the history* (or generations) *of the heavens and the earth when they were created, in the day that the Lord God made the earth and the heavens* (Genesis 2: 4).

This second narrative of creation is a summary of chapter one and refers to what follows, beginning with the history of man and what happens next. This is crucial to our identifying with holiness as it relates to an unadulterated spiritual relationship with God.

Elohim

Is the traditional Hebrew word, used in Jewish teaching to describe God in His creative and judgment role in the universe? In the Genesis account, we see God as the source of all things as He acts in nature creating something out of nothing according to His will. Our understanding of creation is limited in light of God's Word. The order of creation is more important to me than the length of time used to create something. It speaks volumes about a meticulous God who cares about perfection, leaving nothing to chance, in what He provides for all His creation.

Depending upon your interpretation, whether one believes in a literal six day creation or each day a period of time, is of little consequence as long as you believe God is the origin of the universe. In Genesis 1: 5, 8, 13, separates the creation events described as one day each. Some describe the first three days of creation are not ordinary days as the days of man.

According to Jewish teaching recorded in Psalms, some are considered days expressing a span or periods, belonging to God.

Before the mountains were brought forth, Or ever You had formed the earth and the world, Even from everlasting to everlasting, You are God. For a thousand years in Your sight are like yesterday when it is past (Psalms [90: 2, 4])

It is implied then that earthly or human calculations of time do not apply to the first three days of creation because the stars, moon, and sun were not yet in existence. These did not exist until the fourth day alluded to when *Then God said, "Let there be lights in the firmament of the heavens to divide the day from the night; and let them be for signs and seasons, and for days and years"* (Genesis 1: 14).

For example, the stars were to aid man in his travels; the days and seasons regulate the twelve-month calendar dictating planting of seeds and harvest. The Hebrew word for seasons also means "festivals" established according to the seasons of the year.

Regardless of your belief, it makes little sense to cause friction among God's people when each side presents an un-provable explanation. One fact we can all agree on is that, *In the beginning God created* (Genesis 1: 1a).

> **Footnote**: The Hebrew word for day is "Yom" expressed in various lengths of time. *God called the light Day, and the darkness He called Night* (Genesis 1: 5). Each indicates a twelve-hour span of time. In Genesis 1: 14

Moses uses "Yom" expressing a twenty-four hour period. In Genesis, 2: 4 again uses the word "Yom" to explain the entire creative week. In other texts, "Yom" expresses time, years, seasons, and age to mention a few.

Until the creation of man on day Six, the calculation of time according to humankind was of no importance. I believe the creation account so that we can understand it was an orderly creation created by a meticulous God, leaving nothing to chance, although many may disagree.

Adonay

The Hebraic word used to reveal God another way foreseen in His association with humankind. This will affect how we view God concerning our relationship to Him. Here He is referred to as Lord, Master, or Owner in His revelation of Himself to humanity. His love, His mercy, and impartial judgment as the moral ruler of the universe confirm Him in his creation.

It has been said; "that man is the Crown of God's Creation" and differs from all His other creations.

> *Then God said, "let Us make man in Our image, according to Our likeness; let them have dominion over the fish of the sea, over the birds of the air, and over the cattle, over all the earth and over every creeping thing that creeps on the earth"* (Genesis 1: 26).

Let Us make man, describes man as a special creation by God Himself when He formed man from the dust of the earth. God's last work of creation differs from the animals created earlier as He identifies with man, *In Our image, according to Our likeness.* God shaped man to be ageless a likeness of His own eternity.

Man's spiritual nature is potentially divine gifted like his Creator with moral character, and freedom of will. This is a very important concept that has caused much anguish in the church for those who believe in predestination in understanding man's dilemma involving free will and his relationship to God pertaining to man's salvation.

Before we conclude this chapter, I leave you with my final thoughts on creation for consideration. With confidence it is sensible to say, no one will come to terms with the mysteries of creation. Providing one accepts, the first three days cannot literally be equivalent to twenty-four hour periods, because the stars, moon, and sun was yet in existence. Especially since we have limited knowledge-involving time according to man's calculations concerning the first three days of creation and how long it took God to create.

There are mysteries of the universe pertaining to angelic creation, the fall of Satan, numerous galaxies, etc…that man is incapable of understanding. Job chapters thirty-eight through forty-two provide complex insight involving creation illustrated below.

In the final chapters of Job, God proves man has limited knowledge asking Job a series of questions concerning creation.

> *Who is this who darkens counsel By words without knowledge? Now prepare yourself like a man; I will question you, and you shall answer Me. "Where were you when I laid the foundations of the earth? Tell Me, if you have understanding. Who determined its measurements? Surely you know! Or who stretched the line upon it? To what were its foundations fastened? Or who laid its cornerstone, When the morning stars sang together, And all the sons of God shouted for joy? Or who shut in the sea with doors, When it burst forth and issued from the womb; When I made the clouds its garment, And thick darkness its swaddling band; When I fixed My limit for it, And set bars and doors. When I said, This far you may come, but no farther, And here your proud waves must stop"* (Job 38: 2 – 11).

God continues probing Job for answers and in chapter thirty-nine, concludes with His first set of questions by asking; *"Shall the one who contends with the Almighty correct Him? He who rebukes God, let him answer it"* (Job 40: 2). God then follows with more questions and Job finally answered the Lord.

> *I know that You can do everything, And that no purpose of Yours can be withheld from You. You asked, "Who is this who hides counsel without knowledge? Therefore I have uttered what I did not understand, Things too wonderful for me, which I did not know"* (Job 42: 2 – 3).

Job's answer suggests caution be used regarding setting an exact period as some have until we can resolve the mysteries of the universe and understand all the parameters that make up creation. For me it is enough, *In the beginning God created the heavens and the earth* (Genesis 1:1).

As humans, we have a difficult enough time understanding oneself, much less our relationship to God, let alone those intricacies involving creation. Our faith is, often challenged by what we encounter as so-called new evidence supporting some theory involving creation other than what the Bible presents.

An unprovable misconception, astronomers believe the Milky Way is among the oldest of galaxies following the big bang. Their unproven scientific theory puts its age at thirteen-plus billion years, give, or take several hundred million years estimating one-hundred to four-hundred billion stars.

Both Isiah and the Psalmist explain creation by a meticulous Creator leaving nothing to chance.

> *Lift up your eyes on high, And see who has created these things, Who brings out their host by number; He calls them all by name, By the greatness of His might And the strength of His power; Not one is missing* (Isaiah 40: 6). *He counts the number of the stars; He calls them all by name* (Psalms 147: 4).

Unless, we have an authoritative appreciation for God as the "Supreme Creator, Ruler and Judge" of all that He created, we cannot establish the need for holiness for humankind as commanded by God. Additional resources: *The Pentateuch & Haftorahs,* Hebrew Text English Translation & Commentary and *Exploring the Old Testament*, Beacon Hill Press

CHAPTER 3

Beginning of Life
The First Family

The Breathe of life:
And the Lord God formed man of the dust of the ground, and breathed into his nostrils the breath of life; and man became a living being (Genesis 2: 7).

This irrefutably describes man in his actual physical process complete with a heart, soul, and mind enabling him to be a rational living being capable of worship experiencing a close relationship with his Creator.

What is interesting Jesus reiterates man's duty to love God in the same manner today embodying the scriptural truth of holiness taught in both the Old and New Testament. *Jesus said to him, "You shall love the Lord your God with all your heart, with all your soul, and with all your mind"* (Matthew 22: 37.

This spiritual union with God was to be a holy communion without sin describing man in God's spiritual likeness, pertaining to his moral character, *Then God said, "let Us make man in Our image, according to Our likeness"* (Genesis 1: 26).

It is crucial and equally interesting, Eve, was not fashioned like Adam, but formed from Adams rib? Neither Adam nor Eve evolved over a period-of-time, as some presume. Adam formed from the dust of the ground, and Eve created from a rib equal to Adam in all aspects.

Eve's creation as Adams helper was a separate life form following the creation of Adam. The Hebrew for helper is *Kenegdo* signifying the same physical resemblance of each other for mutual companionship. Only a Creator God is capable of such a miraculous act Genesis 2: 18 – 22.

The animals differ from Adam in that they do not possess a soul, nor reflect moral character like their Creator. Incidentally, the animals did not develop over time; but created from the dust like Adam. Therefore, neither could have evolved from the other, nor be an allegory as some believe given the actual time and place to each origin. Only a Creator God could produce such a miracle.

The First Family

When Adam and Eve were both created they were perfect suggests they were mutually alike, physically and spiritually. They were also compatible meaning companionable to each other in their relationship, which was a monogamous relation. *Therefore a man shall leave his father and mother and be joined to his wife, and they shall become one flesh* (Genesis 2: 24).

What is remarkable is the fact this verse appears to be out of context because the family as we know it today was not yet in existence. Some scholars believe that Adam did not say this. The only plausible explanation; Moses led by the Holy Spirit, included this for future generations to follow.

Jesus confirms the union between a man and a woman now becoming as one flesh nurturing each to become closer than their original family. He codifies marriage as a part of an organized system establishing the rule of law when questioned by the Pharisees concerning divorce by quoting the Old Testament.

The purpose of marriage is to preserve and set apart or sanctify that which is, made whole, in the image of God. The woman is to be a help to her husband and the husband is to care and defend his wife as he would defend himself.

Paul in his letter to the Ephesians 5: 22 - 25 instructed the husbands to love their wives just as Christ loved the church. Just as the wife has no greater honor than to love and respect her husband, the husband has no greater duty than to love and protect his wife above his own life.

Several times, in the Old Testament, God used the metaphor of a marriage to describe His bond to Israel. This is a fundamental concept associated with holiness involving one's fidelity to each other. The insincere relations seen in marriages today leading to divorce should serve as a warning. The original bond between a man and a woman had no termination clause in it.

The same rule that pertains to the husband and wife having a monogamist relationship, applies to our relationship to God. This is consistent with the very first commandment; *You shall have no other gods before Me* (Exodus 20: 3). Just as a husband and wife are to be completely devoted to each other, we are to be faithful to God in the same manner. The only way the bond could be broken was by death or infidelity.

Man Created an Intellectual Being

In the Hebrew, the word formed written *vayyitzer* with two *yods*. For that reason, humankind was possessed with a *Yetzer Tob* (the ability to do right) and a *Yetzer Ra* (the ability to commit evil). Morally interpreted means capable of doing both good and evil having to do with one's choice they make.

It is interesting and worthy of note, the animals and creatures created before man have no righteous discrimination or moral conflict. They have only one *yod*. This is why animals can prey on each other, also on humankind without remorse or guilt of conscience.

This being undisputable true relating to animals, makes the human race profoundly different. For this reason, humankind is responsible for his actions and his accountability to God. Because of this man will not have any excuse of wrongdoing before God on the, Day of Judgment. God has provided everything necessary for his salvation. Additional resources: *The Pentateuch & Haftorahs,* Hebrew Text English Translation & Commentary and *Exploring the Old Testament*, Beacon Hill Press..

In concurrence with this, the Psalmist David describes man as being, *made a little lower than the angels and You have crowned him with glory and honor* (Psalms 8: 5). This places humankind at the pinnacle of His creation made in God's image and likeness, and alludes to man's innocence at creation being capable of choice by reason relating to his morals and service to God. The Psalmist implies this in Psalms 8: 6 – 8, where Adam is tending the garden, and having dominion over the animals, birds, and fish of the sea.

Therefore, Adam given control has a direct correlation to our spiritual wellness involving the discipline required for completing the task assigned. The Apostle Paul gives credence to this in his second letter to the Thessalonians where he instructs or warns them against idleness that leads one to becoming a disorderly busybody. Paul emphasizes the importance of work when he wrote, *if anyone will not work, neither shall he eat* (2 Thessalonians 3: 6 – 10 entire text not printed).

Therefore, the statement agrees with Genesis 2: 15 – 16, where Adam receives instructions to tend the garden before he could eat of the fruit with the exception of one tree. Strong work ethics have always been a part of the Christian culture.

This persuasion has nothing to do with salvation through works, as if we can earn our salvation; it has everything to do with being accountable.

Freedom of Choice

Freedom of choice is a wonderful gift and carries with it certain responsibility requiring attention to detail exacting consequences.

> *And the Lord God commanded the man, saying, "of every tree of the garden you may freely eat; but of the tree of the knowledge of good and evil you shall not eat, for in the day that you eat of it you shall surely die"* (Genesis 2: 16 – 17).

You shall not eat gives merit to man's most sacred privilege. This freedom of will or choice reflects his ability to obey or disobey the instructions of His Creator.

God will never violate this sacred privilege. This is not to say that our Lord will not warn us against committing wrong deeds. He will never overrule us as long as we are determined to do otherwise.

Unlike the animals man has a spiritual life accountable to God whose moral laws determines what is good and what is evil not in the devising of man's intellect as seen in our society today. Some advocate there many roads that lead to heaven and each is free to choose his or her path without consequence. Only a small portion of that statement is true, we are "Free to Choose." There is only one way to heaven and that is through Christ Jesus.

Source of Temptation

Temptations can be deadly especially when we yield to its attraction. One's action usually follows some external enticement in our lives. This applies to all human beings without prejudice. These desires affect us in a positive or a negative way based upon the decision we make. Depending upon the circumstance some actions carry a lifetime of regrets.

Sinful habits can cause scars upon one's life for years to come, even after coming to Christ. Wrongful temptations come from only one primal source. James the brother of our Lord makes this clear.

> *Let no one say when he is tempted, "I am tempted by God;" for God cannot be tempted by evil, nor does He Himself tempt anyone. But each one is tempted when he is drawn away by his own desires and enticed. Then, when desire has conceived, it gives birth to sin; and sin, when it is full-grown, brings forth death. Do not be deceived, my beloved brethren. Every good gift and every perfect gift is from above, and comes down from the Father of lights, with whom there is no variation or shadow of turning* (James 1: 13, 17).

Notice the progression temptation takes to snare its prey. It does not occur all at once without warning, but takes place over time, depending upon the nature of the temptation. At first, it may seem innocent with no smell or taste of wrongdoing. A person does not awake one morning and say to self, "I'm going out and steal today."

As an example, oversimplified in today's permissive society, someone may take an item from the workplace without permission believing no wrongs been committed. This logic can lead to other wrongful acts as well.

Temptations are a part of life that we will never outgrow or escape as long as we are in this body. Jesus indicates this in our Lord's Prayer when He instructs us to pray, *do not lead us into temptation, But deliver us from the evil one* (Matthew 6: 9 – 13, entire text not printed).

Our Lord's Prayer suggests two things temptations are real and deliverance promised. Temptation requires a choice to exercise our free will. Do not allow pride to suggest that you can defeat the devil in your own strength.

You should as James instructs, *Therefore submit to God. Resist the devil and he will flee from you* (James 4: 7). Because humankind is empowered with reason, one can control their impulses though difficult at times. We can either abstain from its enticement to commit wrong or yield to the sinful acts suggested. The choice is ours.

Web of Deceit

Deception by any means is still deception no matter how it is sugar coated. The first biblical illustration is in the story of the fall of man in the Garden-of-Eden where Satan weaves his web. Satan is a master at this and on our own we are no match for him as Eve was about to discover.

> *Now the serpent was more cunning than any beast of the field which the Lord God had made. And he said to the woman, "has God indeed said, you shall not eat of every tree of the garden?" And the woman said to the serpent, "we may eat the fruit of the trees of the garden; but of the fruit of the tree which is in the midst of the garden, God has said, you shall not eat it, nor shall you touch it, least you die." Then the serpent said to the woman, "you will not surely die. For God knows that in the day you eat of it your eyes will be opened, and you will be like God, knowing good and evil." So when the woman saw that the tree was good for food, that it was pleasant to the eyes, and a tree desirable to make one wise,*

she took of its fruit and ate. She also gave to her husband with her, and he ate (Genesis 3: 1 – 6).

Several things occurred in these passages of Scripture. First, we note that temptations can come from strange sources to entice us offering up that which is desirable. One would not think of the source of temptation coming from a serpent.

Some Rabbinical Scholars believe that the serpent was superior to the other beasts of the field mainly because of his ability to have the clever ability to carry on a rational alluring conversation with a person, causing them to act against the known will of God.

These same scholars believe that the serpent had a counter motive, the serpent was envious of God's creation of man, and his jealousy caused him to plot man's fall. Satan's aim is to keep people a prisoner to sin and away from God's grace and forgiveness.

No matter the source of temptation, remember James said; "*each one is tempted when he is drawn away by his own desires.*" Eve now engaged in the conversation with the serpent preferring her own intellect adding her own words, *nor shall you touch it,* she began to lose the battle. Eve's response to the serpent, *nor shall you touch it,* actually augments God's original command that God gave Adam.

This expansion or exaggeration of the truth according to the Midrash (the "Midrash" is the ancient homiletically exposition of the Torah), is believed to be the real cause of her fall. This being true, we can conclude that Eve took the bait wanting to acclaim herself in her contest with the serpent.

The serpent boldly denies the validity of God's promise when he told her, *you will not surely die, your eyes will be opened, and you will be like God knowing good and evil.* Eve now looked upon the tree with a new desire of some hidden knowledge beyond her being able to distinguish between right and wrong. Eve caught up in the moment began to assert herself over God, and therefore ignored His command. She turned her back upon her consciousness of truth, gratitude, love, and accountability to God for self-satisfaction. Sound familiar!

We can all learn from Eve's mistake. God made available this truth for our benefit. When we begin to desire our way, over God's will, then God's will moves to the background, and our way comes to the forefront. After a while, the line between obedience and disobedience blurs, as it did with Eve.

Pride is a factor that defeats the Christian in their walk in holiness. Eve obviously demonstrated some pride in her newfound knowledge only to misquote God.

In Matthew 4: 1 – 11, when Jesus was tempted in the wilderness, He never engaged in conversation with Satan with the exception of using God's Word as His defense. Remember, James not only gave us the blueprint of temptation he also instructs us on how to defeat our enemy when tempted.

Naturally the serpent lied, and Adam and Eve were about to find this out. You know the rest of the story, Adam and Eve blew it. They disobeyed God, both ate from the forbidden tree of knowledge, and sin entered the human race changing humankind forever. All too often, what one wishes for never turns out how they want it?

The knowledge received was neither happiness nor wisdom, or control as thought to obtain. They left the garden with only the guilt of sin for company and its collision against the will of God. Sin is never satisfying, and man will always reap what he sow's, as God promised.

Sadly, Adam and Eve were not the last to fall prey to the enemy of our soul. This is why John instructed his followers to *test the spirits, whether they are of God; because many false prophets have gone out into the world* (1 John 4: 1b).

Today there are many *false prophets,* who pretend to be sheep in wolves clothing, seducing well-meaning church members, by providing them with a substitute means to holiness. Their rationale based upon our culture, which is in a constant state of change often suggests that we must redefine Christianity. They promote that a new church should emerge in response to these.

This new church should focus less on traditional teachings for example, truth based upon Scripture, God's grace, repentance involving man's salvation, and adopt a more worldview ideology involving saving our planet, putting an end to earthly social injustices for starters. The strong warning here is any spirit in the flesh or otherwise, that leads you away from Christ is not of God. Be aware of the easy road offered by those who believe all roads lead to heaven.

Be Sure Your Sins Will Find You Out

Adam with no place to go now forced to face God and give a full account of what happened in the garden. Picture Adam and Eve hiding from their Creator when God calls to Adam and asks, *"Where are you"* (Genesis 3: 9b)? Here we see His love in taking the initiative in man's redemption. God is more interested in our wellbeing than we are our self as witnessed by this story. Man can never claim otherwise, and be justified.

God calls Adam out of love to allow him time to seek forgiveness for himself. He is not pressuring Adam but wants him to exercise his free will and make the right choice by acknowledging his sin. We see Adam offering an excuse in his own defense, when he told God, *"Because I was naked"* (Genesis 3: 10b). Many today like Adam, are in denial of wrongdoing.

God then asks Adam, *"Have you eaten from the tree of which I commanded you that you should not eat"* Genesis 3: 11)? Here Adam has an opportunity to give a full confession and show his deep expression of sorrow, but only offers up more excuses. After finding his excuses useless now throws the blame upon everybody but himself including God when he blames the woman that God gave him.

In sound reasoning, a sin not confessed nor repented of or un-atoned is a sin occurring repeatedly. It is only when we acknowledge our sins before God confess them and repent; we can recover from our fallen state through Christ. These steps toward victory are vital if sin is to be defeated in our lives.

Like the alcoholic or drug addict until he acknowledges his dependence to substance abuse he will never recover from his addiction. The Psalmist David declared there is no place man can hide from God, and that God has perfect knowledge of man and all his activities, *Where can I go from Your Spirit? Or where can I flee from Your presence* (Psalms 139: 1 – 12 entire texts not printed)?

CHAPTER 4

Consequence of sin

Sowing and Reaping

Man's Rebellious Nature:
> *For to be carnally minded is death, but to be spiritually minded is life and peace. Because the carnal mind is enmity against God; for it is not subject to the law of God, nor indeed can be* (Romans 8: 6 – 7).

Man's rebellious nature described by the Apostle Paul is a sentence of death. To understand the complex carnal condition we were born with corrupting the human race, without being too repetitive, we need to look again to Genesis at what transpired in the Garden-of-Eden.

To continue living in the carnal state is a sure sign of spiritual condemnation. Apart from the fall, the story of the garden is probably one of the most beautiful stories found in Scripture.

There was Adams miraculous beginning; then his appointment in life as steward over all creatures, ending with his temptation and the consequences following his sin. Paul wrote to the Romans *For as by one man's disobedience many were made sinners* (Romans 5: 19a). This trilogy connecting all humanity is one of the most tragic portrayals of the human race.

Eve's part in the fall of humankind is one of mystery ending with a question mark asking why. One can only speculate about what occurred in the mind of Eve prior to her encounter with the serpent. We have no record of how many times passing by the forbidden tree she looked upon it with increased desire.

The Bible does however make it clear that she looked upon the tree as food pleasing to the eye and yearned for it to make one wise.

There is no biblical evidence she ever shared this hidden desire with Adam.

More often than not, most impulsive actions typically lead to serious unforeseeable consequences as Eve soon discovered. Similar to Adam and Eve a person may often feel justified in their way of behaving regardless of the circumstances, none are exempt.

The consequences of sin are a terrible thing whether one transgresses on purpose or naively ignores their actions at the time. The results are always the same causing embarrassment, shame, and suffering.

Results of Disobedience

Because God is, sovereign, He knows what is best for us in our present state as well with our future. Life in the garden for Adam and Eve was good; God made every provision for their success and happiness as He does for ours. God placed Adam in the Garden to tend it to keep it from growing wild giving him a part in His creation enjoying great pleasure in doing the will of his Father.

God never intended the human race to be idle or lazy. We all heard the old saying, "Idle hands are the devil's workshop." Paul confirms this about those who will not work leading to one called a busybody always getting into trouble 2 Thessalonians 3: 10 – 11.

Far different from today's bustle all Adam and Eve had to do was keep one simple command. This understood was man's first test of obedience and dependence upon God. The first command given to man was *of the tree of the knowledge of good and evil you shall not eat,* followed by the promise *for in the day that you eat of it you shall surely die* (Genesis 2: 17). The instructions were very clear so there could be no misunderstanding between Adam and God.

While God will not violate man's right to choose right or wrong man has an obligation that demands his obedience to the will of God. Adam and Eve was no exception and neither are we. As God promised, two things happened: first a spiritual separation from God becomes apparent severing their sinless relation with God as initially enjoyed in the garden. Second, physical death was inevitable losing the immortality of their physical state here upon earth.

A New Nature Given

Because of Adam's sin their spiritual nature, became, altered. Adam and all of his offspring are now born with this fallen nature. Everyone now possesses a carnal or fleshly nature because both chose to disobey God of their own free will. For this reason, they were no longer subject to the law of God that one must obey Him, *Because the carnal mind is enmity against God* (Romans 8: 7a).

For the same reason, because of our carnal nature, regardless of God's love and provision in Christ we choose our own destiny of either heaven or hell as our eternal resting place. The final decision is ours to either accept Christ or reject Him, John 3: 18, 5: 24, 6: 40, 47.

Separated From God

Several truths regarding sin can be ascertained which are of vital importance to our understanding. As result of their disobedience, they could no longer live in a garden where their livelihood was provided for them. Sin causes man to leave God's presence when we consider that God drove Adam and Eve from the garden, Genesis 3: 22 – 24. Both banished to a wilderness illustrated by their punishment in life.

Their physical expulsion illustrates that a spiritual separation occurs when one transgresses the known will of God. The price of disobedience is costly and not without dire consequences. What was once sweet now become bitter as Solomon points out, *He who sows iniquity will reap sorrow (or trouble)* (Proverbs 22: 8).

From the beginning, Adam's task was to tend the garden, but now his job would become much more difficult. The land would only yield its crop depending upon his unceasing labor. God said, *"Cursed is the ground for your sake; In toil you shall eat of it all the days of your life"* (Genesis 3: 17b).

The sweat of his brow now earns what was once in abundance. Eve like Adam did not escape for her part in being disobedient when God said, *"I will greatly multiply your sorrow and your conception; In pain you shall bring forth children; Your desire shall be for your husband, And he shall rule over you"* (Genesis 3: 16).

Their life of toil and misery would be a constant reminder to them and all of their offspring of their sin and the unhappiness it brings. Humankind having sunk into the mire of sin unable to redeem itself must rise through the spiritual pureness of Christ suffering death upon the cross as promised.

Since Adam, the Scriptures are full of stories of wrongdoing and the punishment brought about because of it. Esau sold his birthright for a bowl of stew or pottage. His inheritance at that moment was not important as the bowl of pottage, Genesis 25: 30 – 34.

Sampson who mocked Delilah about his strength lost his eyesight and forced to pull the grinding stone in shame before his enemies, Judges 6: 6 – 21.

David, because of his moment of pleasure with Bathsheba, and his shedding innocent blood the sword never left his household, 2 Samuel 12: 10.

Sin will cause you to do things you never dreamed possible and carry you further that you ever wanted to go. Sin never brings happiness or joy promised by Satan, only misery in the end. May all these examples serve as a warning?

Physical Death Occurred

In the beginning, God created man to be an immortal being. Because of disobedience, he now became a mortal and the sentence of death was upon him, *For dust you are, and to dust you shall return* (Genesis 3: 19b).

God in His love and mercy postponed the immediate penalty of death because they did not die on the day they ate the forbidden fruit. Their banishment from the Garden-of-Eden proves this.

The first family and all their offspring condemned to slowly die physically determined by their spirits departure, *Then the dust will return to the earth as it was, And the spirit will return to God who gave it* (Ecclesiastes 12: 7).

Had their death occurred on the day of their sin, Adam and Eve would not have had an opportunity to offer any blood sacrifice for their transgression nor there become a human race.

The Bible is silent upon this opinion, the only basis for this belief according to Adam Clarke is the clothing was made from animal skins following their disobedience.

They were likely taken from the animals whose blood was poured out for a sin offering to God initiated by God Himself. Here we see God's love for all of us demonstrated by His act of mercy.

In support of this assumption, the only other explanation is that God must have instructed Adam in the importance of a blood sacrifice. We later see it offered by Abel as a sin offering. Unlike Cain's rejected offering of the field, Abel's offering of blood was accepted. This is the first actual mention of a sacrifice offered to atone for wrongdoing.

Abel acknowledged his depravity and offered the sacrifice of atonement in faith; Cain's offering given without faith, was uncaring and unwilling to acknowledge his sinfulness. Animal sacrifices became a very important part of Israel's worship. These sacrifices all pointed to a time when Christ would come and be the final sacrifice for the remission of sin abolishing animal sacrifices forever.

The First Act of Murder

This new sin nature incited the first act of murder when Cain killed Abel in a rage of jealousy found in the fourth chapter of Genesis. Cain's defense to God for his crime was to pretend that he was not his brother's keeper. Like his parents, Cain accepted no accountability for his actions.

Does this sound familiar in today's society when no one wants to accept responsibility for his or her actions? All too often, it is easier to lay the blame on someone else. This mindset has dulled the conscientiousness of the sinner from the truth about his own sinful nature.

For his disobedience, God put a mark upon Cain that no one should slay him. One can only speculate what the physical mark was that set Cain apart. As punishment, he became a vagabond driven out to wander for the rest of his life fearing an avenger would slay him.

Two things suggested here. First, all vengeance belongs to God and not man. Anyone who sees Cain's mark stands reminded they are capable of committing the same wrongdoing. Therefore, anyone who would kill Cain would suffer God's vengeance seven fold signifying all bloodshed is an abomination to God.

Second, we see God's compassion, protection, and love giving Cain an opportunity to repent. To take Cain's, live prematurely before his appointed time of death, could deprive him of an opportunity to repent.

Sin always brings a response, and leads one make the assumption that God is cruel rather than accept the enormity of his guilt before God. The real danger, this attitude of persecution often blinds one to the mercy of God causing them to focus upon himself or herself as the victim as did Cain.

Because of Cain's cry of anguish acknowledged by his banishment from home, some believe that he was a repentant sinner. All we can say is that it is not impossible.

All Have Sinned

Because of what occurred in the Garden-of-Eden every one of Adam's offspring is born with a carnal nature, no one is exempt. The Psalmist David acknowledges this witnessed by his birth, *Behold I was brought forth in iniquity, and in sin my mother conceived me* (Psalms 51: 5). David is not saying that his birth was an act of sin only that he was born with a sinful or carnal nature.

The Apostle Paul validates this truth in his epistle explaining that none is born without this sin nature, *For all have sinned, and fall short of the glory of God* (Romans 3: 23). He expands upon this in the book of Romans that the carnally minded are dead toward God; and that the spiritually minded have life and peace, Romans 8: 6.

Paul teaches that until a spiritual change occurs humankind in his fallen state, though many deny this, is capable of doing all kinds of wicked things cataloged below.

> *Being filled with all unrighteousness, sexual immorality, wickedness, covetousness, maliciousness; full of envy, murder, strife, deceit, evil-mindedness; they are whispers, backbiters, haters of God, violent, proud, boasters, inventors of evil things, disobedient to parents, undiscerning, untrustworthy, unloving, unforgiving, unmerciful; who, knowing the righteous judgment of God, that those who practice such things are deserving of death, not only do the same, but also approve of those who practice them.* (Romans 1: 29 – 32). *Do you not know that the unrighteous will not inherit the kingdom of God? Do not be deceived, neither fornicators, nor idolaters, nor adulterers, nor homosexuals, nor sodomites, nor thieves, nor covetous, nor drunkards, nor revilers, nor extortioners, will inherit the kingdom of God* (1 Corinthians 6: 9 – 10).

From this list, one can only conclude that human beings left to their own wicked devices are capable of committing the most horrible acts against humanity. Evidence of these atrocities reported in the daily newscast around the world and should come as no surprise.

The Great Commission

In the great commission, Christ made it the church's responsibility to enlighten the sinner to the truth of God's Word concerning their sinful condition not to be confused in man's own sense of right or wrong. To confront these acts of evil we must carry out the great commission to our world. If any change is to occur, the lost must acknowledge their sinful condition as truth. Only then can a spiritual transformation take place.

This truth the world does not want to accept. The great commission is without question Christ's command to His followers before ascending to heaven. To help us understand our mission we need to look at what Jesus had to say about our assigned task.

> And Jesus came and spoke to them, saying, "All authority has been given to Me in heaven and on earth. Go therefore and make disciples of all nations, baptizing them in the name of the Father and of the Son and of the Holy Spirit, teaching them to observe all things that I have commanded you; and lo, I am with you always, even to the end of the age" (Matthew 28: 18 – 20). "Go into all the world and preach the gospel to every creature. He who believes and is baptized will be saved, but he who does not believe will be condemned" (Mark 16: 15 – 16).

Prior to commissioning His disciples Jesus taught them the importance of a timely harvest illustrated by an earthly field ready to yield its crop. *"The harvest truly is great, but the laborers are few; therefore pray the Lord of the harvest to send out laborers into His harvest"* (Luke 10: 2).

The harvest here represents the souls of those who need the truth concerning salvation. The laborers embody those called to work in His vineyard and speak for Christ as His ministers.

At this point, the disciples were not ready to fulfill this command and instructed to wait in Jerusalem until the Holy Spirit comes upon them, that they might receive power.

It is unreasonable for one who has never experienced holiness to lead someone into the same experience. Unlike some standing Armies who often change their operation, the churches mission ("raison d'être," main purpose or reason to exist) has stood for over two-thousand years.

The danger facing churches today is compromise. The foundation that we build upon is changing and not for the good. We are exchanging rock for sand. It would appear that the church has lost its first love of making disciples and are substituting a feel good gospel in its place.

New ideologies replacing the gospel of salvation are taking center stage as the new focal point of worship. They are focusing more on getting in touch with, imagery, fairness, and social injustices rather than the traditional biblical message of salvation, repentance, grace, heaven, or hell. It would appear they find this offensive and outdated for the modern day person to believe.

The apostle Paul best describes one's personal responsibility to make a clean break from sin relating to their spiritual warfare. *Therefore, having these promises, beloved, let us cleanse ourselves from all filthiness of the flesh and spirit, perfecting holiness in the fear of God* (2 Corinthians 7: 1).

CHAPTER 5

Law and Grace

Past vs Present

God's Laws Are True:
> *Blessed is the man who walks not in the counsel of the ungodly, Nor stands in the path of sinners, Nor sits in the seat of the scornful; But his delight is in the law of the Lord, And in His law he meditates day and night* (Psalm 1: 1 – 2).

Some believe the Old Testament law is no longer relevant in today's contemporary church. If you believe this then you are not alone; however, this position requires an answer why not have laws?

God's laws are the unshakable guide to what constitutes good and evil, not man's instincts, his reason, or socially accepted practices as many rely upon today. For the same reason in the ominous hour of temptation, many calls light darkness, and darkness light.

Before you dismiss the law as strictly something of the past listen to what Christ our Lord has to say recorded in Matthew. Jesus confirms the law is still valid and will not become abolished ever.

The Apostle Paul in his letter to the Romans illustrates this truth with reference to his condition confirmed by the law. Paul explains the importance of the law's role in revealing the truth about sin in our lives.

> *Do not think that I came to destroy the Law or the Prophets. I did not come to destroy but to fulfill. For assuredly, I say to you, "till heaven and earth pass away, one jot or one tittle will by no means pass from the law till all is fulfilled. Whoever therefore breaks one of the least of these commandments, and teaches men so, shall be called least in the kingdom of heaven; but whoever does*

and teaches them, he shall be called great in the kingdom of heaven" (Matthew 5: 17 – 19). *What shall we say then? "Is the law sin? Certainly not! On the contrary, I would not have known sin except through the law. For I would not have known covetousness unless the law had said, you shall not covet"* (Romans 7: 7).

Without Partiality

The Laws of the Old Testament and Grace in the New Testament complement each other not to the contrary. There never were one standard in former times under the Law and a different standard in the present day under Grace. This will become evident as the chapter unfolds.

God's plan is not dependent upon man; more accurately, man is dependent upon God. The plan of deliverance did not come about by human initiative but by divine appointment.

For one to benefit from God's redemptive plan there are a number of principles found in the Old Testament that agree with the teachings in the New Testament illuminating the way to holiness. The Scriptures unveil a supernatural power that ties both periods together without partiality.

Jesus Christ is the same yesterday, today, and forever (Hebrews 13: 8). If Jesus were not the same yesterday, today, and forever neither He nor the gospel would be consistent. Those judged in the Old Testament would be different from those in the New Testament.

In the Old Testament until Christ could come to earth and fulfill His mission as savior, there had to be a substitute blood sacrifice offering for sin. This came about in the sacrifices of animals on the Day of Atonement when the yearly sin offering for all the children of Israel was prepared.

The Day of Atonement marked the one day the high priest entered the Holy of Holies to offer the sacrificial blood sin offering for the people. This offering provided the atonement for one's sins under the law involving fasting, repentance, and restitution.

When Jesus came and shed His blood for our sins, He cancelled the blood sacrifice of animals forever. He became the living sacrifice by His death, burial, and resurrection. To have an unrelated standard of conduct for both "pre-cross and post-cross" generations would give someone reason to blame God as partial preferring one to the other, which is incorrect.

The Scriptures are very clear on this matter according to the Apostle Paul and Peter. *For there is no partiality with God* (Romans 2: 11). *In truth I perceive that God shows no partiality* (Acts 10: 34).

Old Testament Law

The Old Testament law is essential in defining Christian behavior pertaining to moral living. To shed light on our understanding of their overall value I have divided them into three parts: (1) Commandments (2) Statutes (3) Customs and Traditions. Though interconnected these are not complex in nature with one category looked upon more respected than the others.

Incidentally, the same laws that are applicable to the church should apply to society as the Bible instructs. One assembly should complement the success of the other not to the determent as we are witnessing today. Elected officials are expected to be *God's ministers to you for good, not evil* (Romans 13: 1 - 7 text not printed). Laws provide a balance to aid all mortals in their social and moral living.

Commandments

Commandments include any demand given by God reflecting His righteousness. Commands usually proceed with thou shall, or shall not followed by the demand instructions. These are an obligation and not an option to disobey. All valid commandments should be biblically grounded. The most familiar examples of these reflect the Ten Commandments governed by God's sovereign righteous moral principles Exodus 20: 1 – 17.

The first four clearly based upon our relationship with God. The remaining six have to do with our relationship to each other. If we do not keep the first four, it is impossible to keep the last six. This is why animal sacrifices for sin offerings became part of Israel's worship. The Israelites were powerless, to keep the commandments in their own strength, nor can we.

The standard expressed in the law summarizes our relationship with God and our fellow inhabitants. Jesus authenticated this truth by summing it up this way when asked,

> *"Teacher, which is the great commandment in the law?" Jesus said to him, "You shall love the Lord your God with all your heart, with all your soul, and with all your mind. This is the first and great commandment. And the second is like it: You shall love your neighbor as yourself. On these two commandments hang all the Law and the Prophets"* (Matthew 22: 36 – 40).

Statutes

Statutes are decrees ordained by God that we are to observe though human reason cannot define why. An example would be why some animals considered unclean and some were not; for instance, the Jews were forbidden to eat pork. Just because we cannot understand why God commands such does not exempt us from being obedient in keeping His Word.

A person obeying the law and observing the ceremonies as instructed by God reflects one's willingness to follow God in careful submission reflecting holiness. Enlarging upon this Jesus taught the love for God and love for our neighbor goes beyond the mere exercise of just keeping rules.

> *So the scribe said to Him, "Well said, Teacher. You have spoken the truth, for there is one God, and there is no other but He. And to love Him with all the heart, with all the soul, and with all the strength, and to love one's neighbor as oneself, is more than all the whole burnt offerings and sacrifices." Now when Jesus saw that he answered wisely, He said to*

him, "You are not far from the kingdom of God" (Mark 12: 32 - 34a).

The scribes like many today were so close to the truth yet missing the mark. It is not about works or simply keeping rules we may not understand, rather it is by the Grace of God. This does not minimize our responsibility to keep moral rules. The disciples showed their love for God by keeping His Word.

Our commitment of love and obedience to God's Word is greater than any superficial sacrifice that we might offer or make.

Customs and traditions

Typically, customs and traditions handed down from one generation to the next more often than not influence the teaching of the church. Religious customs and traditions should always align with God's Word or not be practiced. The, *Midrash,* is a Jewish commentary on biblical text, and is a prime example expounding the first five books of Moses.

In Judaism there six hundred thirteen Mitzvot or diktat categorizing the things you should do and the things you should not do before God. They list two hundred forty-eight positive things to do and three hundred sixty-five negative things you should abstain from doing.

All six hundred thirteen commands found in the Torah were, established for a particular purpose based upon a specific Scripture. The book of Leviticus contains the most, second is Deuteronomy, and in third place is Exodus. It only makes sense that Leviticus would contain the most when you consider that Leviticus meaning Law of the Priests or that pertaining to the Levites.

The Jewish people following the destruction of the Second Temple by Titus in seventy-AD cannot observe many of the six hundred thirteen instructions today. The Temple had stood for four hundred twenty years as a sacred place of worship for God's chosen people.

Today there are fewer than one hundred ninety-four positive commandments of things to observe by modern Judaism compared to two hundred forty-eight initially. In contrast, there are seventy-seven negative regulations you should abstain from doing weighed against the former three hundred sixty-five. Consequently, only twenty-six of these apply within the modern state of Israel itself.

As a results one can see the difficulty modern Jewish people encounter in worship according to the established customs of their past. Do not think of such practices as outdated or unimportant. Their observance of these laws reflects their obedience to how they perceive living a holy life in submission to God's command to keep the Sabbath holy.

We can learn a lot from this. This is why it is so important for the Jewish people to rebuild the temple. For additional information, concerning the six hundred thirteen Mitzvot can be found using *Wikipedia,* the online free encyclopedia.

Before we leave this segment, a secular viewpoint involving societies moral laws are vital to the survival of any nation and are two-fold in nature. Without respect, people would pursue anything that suited their desire with no regard to the other person.

This would fuel chaos beyond belief witnessed by those not keeping the law as seen in the Old Testament, *Everyone did what was right in his own eyes* (Judges 21: 25b).

This should serve as an example to any society who behaves in such a way becomes a civilization of the fittest, suggesting only the strongest will survive.

A lesser yet just as deadly sin is when a society becomes more than usually permissive. Both extremes are dangerous and can lead to the downfall of any culture regarding their beliefs, practices, or social behavior.

Laws in themselves are powerless and are only as beneficial as the people who keep them. You cannot protect people from themselves against their will. That is why societies must have laws and enforcement. Churches are no exception.

Based upon your experience have we in the twenty-first century become too casual in what we believe socially about morals or how we worship? If your answer is yes, what can we do to improve? Today many Christians do not take their worship of God serious enough especially pertaining to holiness and holy living.

God's Grace is Essential

It is only by grace through Christ that someone can truly be, liberated. In agreement with grace, the law exposes sin in the life of the sinner and becomes his school master regarding right and wrong. Paul confirms that the law is holy in that it polices ones behavior by rule of authority and condemns the sinful acts of the transgressor Romans 7: 7.

After sin is exposed then grace makes forgiveness possible. Grace enables a person to do what the law could not accomplish, *For by grace you have been saved through faith, and that not of yourselves; it is the gif of God* (Ephesians 2: 8).

The Psalmist David credits all of his being to a likeness of grace attributed to the mercy of God who directs him in all his ways so that he does not go astray, *It is God who arms me with strength, and makes my way perfect* (Psalm 18: 32).

John similarly wrote the same thing with different emphasis quoting the words of our Lord, *I am the vine, you are the branches. He who abides in Me, and I in him, bears much fruit; for without Me you can do nothing* (John 15: 5).

John shows that grace is a partnership initiated by God. It is that unseen act of God apart from any works of man making it possible for man to believe in a sovereign God's mercy without charge.

Grace like the law can be explained using several terms, such as; Prevenient Grace, Saving Grace, and Continual Grace applied in the life of the believer. Grace is a gift from God showing infinite love and mercy allowing man to accomplish what he otherwise is incapable of achieving by any other means.

It is the condition of being set free from sin through repentance on man's part and forgiveness on God's part.

Prevenient Grace

Has been expressed as "going before or preceding" some spiritual activity. Grace is necessary to enlighten the soul to its sinful reality, and convert the unbeliever in the light of truth revealed in the law. God's initial grace prepares the soul to move forward toward God as a repentant sinner and accept Christ as his or her savior.

Because of man's freedom of choice determines the outcome whether or not God's divine grace through Christ's atonement for our sins is accepted or rejected. In other words, man must choose between Christ and sin.

Humankind can no longer ride the fence; they must make their choice for good or evil just as Joshua challenged the children of Israel in his farewell address, *Choose for yourselves this day whom you will serve* (Joshua 24: 15a). Joshua gave them a choice; they could serve the false gods their fathers served, or worship the one true God. We too must choose between Christ and sin. Grace makes it possible.

Saving Grace

Is an extension or continuum of prevenient grace! It is that seamless co-operation between the sinner's journey toward repentance, and grace extended to the unsaved until actual repentance takes on faith making possible our salvation. *For by grace you have been saved through faith, and that not of yourselves; it is the gift of God* (Ephesians 2: 8).

Grace then provides the link between repentance and faith as the final condition of our salvation enabled under the influence of the Holy Spirit. Without the Holy Spirit, none of this would be possible. It is the Holy Spirit, who bears the truth about man's condition and reveals Christ as our personal Savior.

Continual or Sustaining Grace

It is through God's divine intervention, *not of yourselves,* that we are, sustained in our Christian walk. Our faith in Christ in our daily walk is the direct results of God's continual grace seen in His promise

My grace is sufficient for you, for My strength is made perfect in weakness (2 Corinthians 12: 9a). This enables man to have continuous faith although God never forces man to exercise his faith; the power to act remains his choice.

We can conclude then that the law arrests the guilty brings the transgressor to trial and finds him culpable of sin worthy of death. Then Christ, our advocate through grace comes along pleads our case to the Father who pardons the sinner and sets the condemned free without charge as if no crime was ever committed.

Nowhere else in this world will you find that kind of mercy. The only request in return is that you live a life worthy of the sacrifice made in your place.

Understanding the Law through Grace by Faith

Given that we are instructed to *Abstain from every form of evil* (1 Thessalonians 5: 22), could lead someone to believe that it simply requires keeping rules. The truth often misunderstood requiring one to abstain from something is not to be associated with salvation by works.

Today, as in the early church there is confusion or misunderstanding between works under the law and self-discipline according to faith by means of grace. Law and works does not oppose grace by faith.

To live a holy life worthy of the sacrifice that was made in our place suggests that we must be busy performing something. You can never achieve holiness by simply keeping rules governing our conduct. It goes much deeper than that. *Abstain from every form of evil* compels a response by the redeemed that requires a separated life counter to the world's life style.

James, who many scholars believe to be the brother of our Lord puts it in perspective and demonstrates its achievability. There is a correlation between works and faith working in unison with the follower of Christ. The two acts much in the same manner as a marriage.

> *What does it profit, my brethren, if someone says he has faith but does not have works? Can faith save him? Thus also faith by itself, if it does not have works, is dead. But someone will say, You have faith, and I have works. Show me your faith without works, and I will show you my faith by my works. For as the body without the spirit is dead, so faith without works is dead also* (James 2: 14, 17 - 18, 26).

James is not saying that our salvation is by works or simply in keeping the law. He pools the two truths together that most clearly reflect the teaching of Christ concerning the greatest of the commandments, when was asked the question by a lawyer.

> *Jesus said to him, "You shall love the Lord your God with all your heart, with all your soul, and with all your mind. This is the first and great commandment. And the second is like it: You shall love your neighbor as yourself"* (Matthew 22: 37 - 39).

Our lives must reflect the truth to love God in heaven and to love man on earth as Jesus instructs. We can deduce then that works and faith support each other in keeping holiness active so that our spiritual lives will not become vain or imaginary *For as the body without the spirit is dead, so faith without works is dead also* (James 2: 26). The connection here suggests that one without the other becomes selfish and unproductive.

Keeping our Conscience Clear

Keeping our conscience clear is important in safeguarding our spiritual walk. Often our conscience bothers us probed by the question am I doing wrong in obeying the rule of law (or works) at the expense of grace; or am I superimposing the gospel of grace commencing the surrender of works?

To the careful reader understanding these difficult concepts are crucial when attempting to connect the spiritual application to our lives between Old Testament Judaism and New Testament Christianity that James wrote about in his letter.

When difference of opinion occur with matters of our conscience concerning faith by grace or keeping the law we need to keep the two separate in our thinking. Martin Luther (1483 – 1546) that great Reformer, Monk, Professor, Scholar, and Author illustrated it something like this in his writings.

He used two opposite boundaries to describe the relationships between the law, and Scriptures have and how they affect the follower of Christ. Simply stated the gospel belongs in heaven while the law is associated with earth.

When dealing with matters of conscience regarding faith we need to set aside momentarily the law and let it stay on earth and seek agreement with the gospel in heaven as the Scripture teaches *For in it the righteousness of God is revealed from faith to faith; as it is written, 'The just shall live by faith"* (Romans 1: 17).

When in dispute with our conscience on how we are to live out our life here upon earth concerning our actions, we need to consult the law. In order to do this one must find a sense of balance by keeping their conscience clear with compliance to the law to support grace.

Jesus in His sermon on the mount gave us good instructions concerning our earthly duty toward others reflecting good works *Therefore, whatever you want men to do to you, do also to them, for this is the Law and Prophets* (Matthew 7: 12).

To conclude then, while on earth the Christian is to do the work of Him who saved and sanctified them. They can only do this through faith in Christ's righteousness of grace and not in one's own strength as Paul wrote, *... be found in Him, not having my own righteousness, which is from the law, but that which is through faith in Christ, the righteousness which is from God by faith* (Philippians 3: 9).

CHAPTER 6

Holiness God's Commandment

Rags to Riches

Holiness is Attainable:

Pursue peace with all people, and holiness, without which no one will see the Lord (Hebrews 12: 14).

Many often overlook this verse, despite the fact that it implies we are to strive for a peaceful coexistence with those around us. We are to live holy in a continual life of heart purity separated from the worldly pleasures that God condemns in His Word. Without holiness, no one will see God establishes an obvious, unambiguous requirement to gain a heavenly entrance into the presence of God.

Yesterday and Today

Some accept as fact that God has different requirements judged differently for the Old and New Testament periods relating to how people are to live in the world. Declaring both truths Leviticus and 1 Thessalonians support the same obligation for moral living.

The Scriptures are comparable in meaning equally identical in purpose with regard to heart purity mutually expressing parallel divine truths.

For I am the Lord your God. You shall therefore consecrate yourselves, and you shall be holy; for I am holy. And the Lord spoke to Moses, saying, "Speak to all the congregation of the children of Israel, and say to them: You shall be holy, for I the Lord your God am holy" (Leviticus 11: 44a, 19: 1 – 2). *For this is the will of God, your sanctification: that you should abstain from sexual immorality; that each of you should know how to possess his own vessel in sanctification and honor, not in passion of*

> *lust, like the Gentiles who do not know God. For God did not call us to uncleanness, but in holiness. Therefore he who rejects this does not reject man, but God, who has also given us His Holy Spirit* (1 Thessalonians 4: 3 - 5, 7 – 8).

The word, *Consecrate* (some translations uses sanctify) under the law literally means to personally strive after perfection or holiness. In the Old Testament reflected achieving holiness by works or keeping the law, and through grace in the New Testament. The phrase, *all the congregation* was required for all the people of Israel, not just a select few such as prophets and priests. It was a deliberate act of the people themselves to, willingly submit, to God as a vessel used according to His will.

Paul, in his letter to the Thessalonians, reintegrated these truths from the past involving one's responsibility and obligation to seek holiness, confirming the universal requirement for all people. The expression, *he who rejects this does not reject man, but God* confirms to reject holiness carries the same penalty if to reject God. Compounding the matter, to reject God you reject His sovereign Word and engage in an aggressive act refusing to take part or become involved in the holiness process.

The declaration *who has given us His Holy Spirit,* clearly defines how the New Testament early church received these truths, again emphasizing, that to reject these truths was in reality rejecting God not man. The presence of the Holy Spirit in our lives guarantees all the follower of Christ, that righteousness be obtained, and sustained.

It is unthinkable to believe that God has an unattainable standard for His people or would require something without providing the means to achieve. The Apostle Paul's restates this Old Testament truth of consecration to the early church, and instructs all believers to do the same.

I beseech you therefore, brethren, by the mercies of God, that you present your bodies a living sacrifice, holy, acceptable to God, which is your reasonable service (Romans 12: 1). A person's devotion to

God regardless of who we are requires the same sacrificial commitment to faithful living.

Royal Command

To expand our understanding of the Old Testaments fundamental dynamics of holiness and how it saturated the lives of the Israelites; we need to examine a very important passage that has long been referred to as Israel's "Watchword and Confession of Faith" known as the "Shema," *Hear, O Israel: The Lord our God, the Lord is one! You shall love the Lord your God with all your heart, with all your soul, and with all your strength* (Deuteronomy 6: 4 – 5).

The instructions, *Hear, O Israel: The Lord our God, the Lord is one* enshrines Judaism's greatest contribution to the religious importance for the human race. These words sum up the teaching of the First and Second Commandments of God, declaring that He alone is God who wholly deserves our praise and worship. According to Jewish tradition every other sacred belief circumvolved around it; all originate from it; all return to it.

The remaining segment of the Shema, *You shall love the Lord your God with all your heart, with all your soul, and with all your strength* in simple language translates, we should give God our total undivided allegiance. We must be willing to surrender our most treasured wishes and inclinations for the love of God. We must be eager to be His ambassador in the service of our Creator.

In body and soul, we must be "unconditionally" His without exception. Jesus Himself confirms this truth when asked by a lawyer; if this remained the greatest Commandment for men to keep.

> *Jesus said to him, "you shall love the Lord your God with all your heart, with all your soul, and with all your mind. This is the first and great commandment. And the second is like it: You shall love your neighbor as yourself. On these two commandments hang all the law and the prophets"* (Matthew 22: 37 – 40).

Longevity of Holiness

Because the Shema was the pivotal thought of Jewish belief, the importance of the teaching reflecting its total obedience is when God instructs the children of Israel to teach these to their offspring.

> *And these words which I command you today shall be in your heart. You shall teach them diligently to your children, and shall talk of them when you sit in your house, when you walk by the way, when you lie down, and when you rise up. You shall bind them as a sign on your hand, and they shall be as frontlets between your eyes. You shall write them on the doorposts of your house and on your gates* (Deuteronomy 6: 6 – 9).

These words which I command you today, conveys do not regard these divine instructions as ancient or yesterdays' news to be outdated or discarded, but consider them fresh as a new "Royal Mandate" renewed daily. *Teach them diligently* literally means to reiterate the Shema, repeatedly, so that its truth remains indelibly inscribed upon the heart.

The Shema became the soul stirring self- expression of Israel's spiritual identity. The recital of the confession of faith was a vital part of their regular daily worship in the temple. When reciting these words, every thought is excluded other than God's oneness.

Worship then, is with the singleness of heart, soul, and mind, and not be interrupted by anyone or anything. They taught that if the words of the confessor, were uttered devoutly and reverently, their very soul would be brought into communion with the Most High.

The recital became the first prayer of early childhood and the last prayer of the dying. This daily reminder of God became Israel's strength, as should be ours. The statement of faith cited by the Israelites is a lot like John 3: 16, one of the most quoted verses in the Christian Bible. Additional resources: *The Pentateuch & Haftorahs,* Hebrew Text English Translation & Commentary

It is then safe to say that holiness dominates the moral and religious teachings found in the Bible. The word holy in the sacred sense stands for the fullness of "God's perfectness" and complete freedom from everything that makes man's conduct impure and imperfect.

What is interesting the same word holy in the ritual or ceremonial custom also means consecrated for religious purposes. This applies to persons and utensils connected with the sanctuary.

To conclude, because of the prerequisite God places upon holiness, in one syllable we cannot allow it to "die." It is important one should have a clear understanding and not a confused or confounded knowledge of the duties and teachings of their faith. It should pass from one generation to the next, without respect of persons.

Noticeably there is something grossly lacking today, reading the Bible is becoming less important among many Christians. The reading and teaching of God's Word becomes paramount to the survival of holiness.

Worshipping God is serious business and never to be taken carelessly. We should strive toward a purity that is divine by keeping away from everything that is wicked or shameful; and for that reason distinguish that we belong to God.

God was not saying that we could ever attain or be like Him in His attributes: Omnipresence, Omniscience, or Omnipotence, but we could obtain certain moral qualities that reflect Him.

Imitation of God

In the Old Testament, man was not only to worship God, but was to imitate Him in their lifestyle. Their lives were to be a carbon copy of their Creator reflecting His moral character. Nothing that suggested even the least corrupt can be associated with God.

They believed because they are, commanded, to be holy carries a dual responsibility, one positive and the other negative. The positive is; they are to emulate God, and keep His laws and do the right things. The negative and most difficult to achieve was the withdrawal from things impure and loathsome, and not to do the things you should abstain.

It was the duty of every Israelite to strive as was attainable under the law, whether it was physical or spiritual to avoid whatever would defile them and keep them from living holy lives. *For I am the Lord your God, you shall therefore consecrate yourselves, and you shall be holy; for I am holy {some translations uses the words sanctify in place of consecrate}* (Leviticus 11: 44).

The intention of imitating God may have had its' roots in the Old Testament it also found its way into the New Testament. Paul's letters to the Ephesians and Philippians gives support to this.

> *Therefore be imitators of God as dear children* (Ephesians 5: 1). *Let this mind be in you which was also in Christ Jesus, who being in the form of God, did not consider it robbery to be equal with God* (Philippians 2: 5 – 6).

For amenable reason, appropriately imitating God is no way robbing God of what rightfully belongs to Him. To the contrary, we are ascribing to God what is His already.

Jesus' our example while here upon earth was to glorify God through His life, and do the work that He was to accomplish. Our role is to emulate that of a servant as Christ taught His disciples, pointing out our Lord's interest now becomes our interest.

This is a reminder, when one looks into a mirror to abstain from evil practices and immoral conduct. I have confidence this infers to our ability to live a holy life.

A Kingdom of Priests

By now, you may be wondering why the reason for a holiness people proclaiming God's will for humankind. Moses gives us one answer ... *you shall be to Me a kingdom of priests and a holy nation. These are the words which you shall speak to the Children of Israel* (Exodus 19: 6).

According to the Old Testament this command refers to a kingdom whose citizens are all priests living wholly in God's service, as servants of God, enjoying the proper access to Him. This was Israel's highest mission, and is our great commission.

It is the duty of every Christian to bring man nearer to God. For Israel, the thought behind the words *a holy nation* means separated from the false teachings and idolatry of the nations around them. In this relationship, Israel became holy by cleaving unto God and obeying His law.

The Apostle Peter, confirms that same mission for the early believers when writing to the church, *You also, as living stones, are being built up a spiritual house, a holy priesthood, to offer up spiritual sacrifices acceptable to God through Jesus Christ* (1 Peter 2: 5).

From the Old to the New Testament the end goal remains the same, *a holy priesthood.* In our day as in previous times, the work continues, our mission is to enlighten the world by showing the world our redeemer Christ our Lord. The believer in Christ is both salt and light to a lost and dying world.

> *You are the salt of the earth; but if the salt loses its flavor, how shall it be seasoned? It is then good for nothing but to be thrown out and trampled underfoot by men. You are the light of the world. A city that is set on a hill cannot be hidden. Nor do they light a lamp and put it under a basket, but on a lamp stand, and it gives light to all who are in the house. Let your light so shine before men, that they may see your good works and glorify your* Father *in heaven* (Matthew 5: 13 – 16).

Role Models Needed

We are living in a day when this generation more than ever needs heroes or role models to look up to. A Godly role model in the daily course of life's events correlates with the holy priesthood that Peter challenged the early church to be.

We live in a time when people are finding it difficult to experience any measure of satisfaction in life. Perhaps this is why many are suicidal, or turning to substances like alcohol and drugs for their comfort. Our world is full of anxiety, worry, and frustration by young and old alike.

Hospital beds are full of people who are emotionally and mentally disturbed, and crime is an all-time high. Many are not happy with their jobs, their bosses, or their partners in life. Others are not happy with their lifestyle, even their own church, and the list goes on.

What is sad but true the church parallels with the world in the divorce rate depending upon your source. This is where holiness, (light) can do the most good in contrast to those described who walks in (darkness).

All too often sports figures, entertainers, or public officials do not fill the bill or match the role. Their lives often filled with scandals eliminating them as candidates.

When you think of a hero or role model what comes to mind? Better yet, who comes to mind? Who in your life made the big difference in leading you to Christ, was it a young person, younger than you were, or was it an older person? No doubt, they were older.

A hero is someone often admired and emulated, for his or her achievements and qualities. Heroes can be real like a decorated soldier or a mythological character like Hercules or a legendary figure like Robin Hood. Unlike role models, heroes usually are the central figure in an event for short period-of-time then disappears.

In complete opposite to a hero a role model takes center stage. The big difference, a role model is a part played out in real life before a live audience open to moral scrutiny without limitations every day.

A synonym that best describes the word model is *exemplar* that suggests someone worthy of imitating. Sad there are few that we can look to that meets that standard in the secular world, but what about the church world. The churches greatest role model to emulate is our Lord and Savior just as Paul instructed Titus to be an example.

> *In all things showing yourself to be a pattern of good works; in doctrine showing integrity, reverence, incorruptibility, sound speech that cannot be condemned, that one who is an opponent may be ashamed, having nothing evil to say of you* (Titus 2: 7 – 8)

On a personal note, I still remember the person who made an indelible impression upon me as a young lad. He was a Nazarene holiness pastor. As a sinner thinking, "If I ever get religion I want the kind Reverend Cooper has."

He was a spiritual role model that influenced me for Christ. In his presence there was a peace about him, that left a person wanting the same. He was the type of person you liked being around. His prayers and influence was instrumental in becoming a Christian.

There are too many today who have shrugged off their responsibility as a role model for too long. Sad to say but true, the only way the world will ever see Christ is our being an example of Christ to the world.

One is never surprised, sometime shocked, at what a sinner might do. However, am stunned at what some Christians do. Allow me to close this chapter with this challenge, as a role model our lives should reflect these truths:

Enlightenment – The world must see there is a difference.

Deliverance – They must believe that a change can take place.

Inheritance – They must believe that a better life is possible in the now and hereafter. What better way to achieve this than through a life of holiness.

CHAPTER 7

God's Blueprint
Road to Success

This is The Way:
> *Your ears shall hear a word behind you, saying, "This is the way, walk in it, Whenever you turn to the right hand Or whether you turn to the left. Whosoever walks the road, although a fool, Shall not go astray"* (Isaiah 30: 21, 35: 8b).

God has a predominate plan for our life, revealed in His Word to live a holy life and enjoy unlimited fellowship with Him. Anything less than this is undesirable. The Master Architect and Builder, has not left us without instructions, support or guidance in our earthly pilgrimage.

To help us identify with holiness, sometimes referred to as righteous living, we need to understand some basic terminology, which I label "God's blueprint." They will aid us with these biblical truths. With any blueprint, the master architect has a design in mind reflected in his drawings categorized as a two-step process.

The drawings and material designed of such that a builder can physically duplicate it in a tangible way. Second, the architect is involved throughout the entire process until completion to ensure nothing goes wrong. I believe we can apply this same analogy to one's spiritual journey in life. In fact, the way is so plain, *although a fool, Shall not go astray*.

In understanding these rudiments, will help us in obtaining the experience of sanctification in our lives. Holiness identified as Christian perfection, perfect love, complete salvation, and entire sanctification is not to be confused with or imply that one never makes an unintentional mistake. The expressions used are to articulate the fullness of salvation conveying the completeness of the Christian character. These unique spiritual graces outlined in the following examples of Scripture.

Consecration

Consecration is an important step toward obtaining Christian perfection. According to these instructions, this action is representational for complete service to God.

> *And he brought the second ram, the ram of consecration. Then Aaron and his sons laid their hands on the head of the ram, and Moses killed it. Also he took some of the blood and put it on the tip of Aaron's right ear, on the thumb of his right hand, and on the big toe of his right foot* (Leviticus 8: 22 – 23).

In the first verse of chapter eight and following, the Lord spoke to Moses giving detailed instructions concerning Aaron and his sons regarding what must transpire. The devotion to God regardless of who we are requires the same dedication or consecration to holy living.

The first part of the ritual prior to consecration was the sacrifice of a bull for the *sin offering* to cleanse the priests of any transgression they may have committed. Until this part was completed, they were unable to offer themselves to God in consecration. This same truth holds applicable today.

The second animal a ram sacrificed as a *burnt offering* embodies the idea of communion with God. This signifies the total surrender in submission of the worshipper to the will of God reflected in his obedience. The *ram of consecration,* a part of the *burnt offering,* involves the act of consecration. Before the final commitment, everything that proceeded established the foundation for induction of the priest by Moses under God's direction.

The phraseology right ear, right thumb, and big toe signify the consecration of the whole person in word, thought, and deed. All that follows our consecration as an act of God, results in our willingness to submit to the Lordship of Jesus Christ. Our willingness to submit our self unconditionally without reservation to the service of God implies a question mark (?) defined by this unselfish act of consecration upon the consecrated. Therefore, only the individual involved can answer this question, are we or are we not, unquestionably His?

Separation

The key meaning in separation implies to come apart, to be different from the world. We cannot serve two masters *God and mammon* as our Lord taught in Matthew 6: 24. Jesus taught that we either love one and hate the other or be loyal to one and despise the other. There is no middle ground in which to stand.

The Apostle Paul describes one's separation depicting their state or condition of Godlikeness.

> *Do not be unequally yoked together with unbelievers. For what fellowship has righteousness with lawlessness? And what communion has light with darkness? And what accord has Christ with Belial? Or what part has a believer with an unbeliever? And what agreement has the temple of God with idols? For you are the temple of the living God. As God has said: "I will dwell in them and walk among them. I will be their God, and they shall be My people. Come out from among them and be separate, says the Lord. Do not touch what is unclean, and I will receive you"* (2 Corinthians 6: 14 – 17).

Do not be unequally yoked together with unbelievers is a warning not to leave the Christian fellowship, and become entangled again immorally by joining the ranks of the sinful. This does not prevent the Christian from witnessing to the unsaved; however, it will not allow him or her to take part in their idolatrous and sinful ways again.

We are to live different life styles or risk being labeled as those having known the way and turned aside are like, *A dog returns to his own vomit* (2 Peter 2: 22b).

Sanctification

The Israelites believe the foundation for sanctification is in the expression to be like God, *You shall be holy; for I am holy* (Leviticus 11: 44). The New Testament agrees our commitment to come apart, to sanctify or separate one's self, is a prerequisite for their capacity to receive the Holy Spirit in His fullness.

> *Abstain from every form of evil. Now may the God of peace Himself sanctify you completely; and may your whole spirit, soul, and body be preserved blameless at the coming of our Lord Jesus Christ. He who calls you is faithful, who also will do it* (1 Thessalonians 5: 22 – 24).

Notice the similarity of *your whole spirit, soul, and body* to the Shema in the Old Testament. *You shall love the Lord your God with all your heart, with all your soul, and with all your strength* (Deuteronomy 6: 4 – 5). The symmetry between these two passages confirms the depth of devotion to God that is required in order to live a righteous and proper life.

In real terms, this translates that we must be wholly His without reservations. The work of sanctification includes both the human act of consecration and God's Divine act of cleansing. Sanctification begins in regeneration (being saved), and is completed in our separation or full surrender or consecration before receiving the Holy Spirit in His fullness.

Law vs. Grace

It is important to understand the arguments between the weakness of the "Law" of the Old Testament; and strength of "Grace" in the New Testament, and how each applies. An appreciation of these is imperative in order to see if holiness is attainable and how they relate to one's spiritual experience.

Paul in his letter to the Romans defines the differences of these two principles and makes it clear in their application.

> *For what the law could not do in that it was weak through the flesh, God did by sending His own Son in the likeness of sinful flesh, on account of sin: He condemned sin in the flesh, that the righteous requirement of the law might be fulfilled in us who do not walk according to the flesh but according to the spirit* (Romans 8: 3 – 4).

He is not saying that people could not strive in keeping the law, though difficult, only that the law was weak and could not fulfill its role by itself.

Because of this flaw, as instructed by God, the priests must continually offer up animal sacrifices as a sin offering for the people. Blood sacrifices of animals were temporary, until the permanent sacrifice of Christ's blood offered for our sins once and for eternity.

When Christ came and died for our sins, He paid the ultimate price. He condemned sin in the flesh for those who repent and accept Him as their savior. Christ's death on Calvary put an end to animal sacrifices under the law forever.

Consequently, keeping the law by doing good deeds, though noble, cannot save a person they must come to Christ. The path to hell is paved with good intentions. God never asks anything of us that He has not provided the resources to achieve according to His purpose and plan.

When we think of grace, it is the unmerited favor of God toward man allowing him to believe and act according to the will of God. In the book of Zechariah and Hebrews, we have an insight how achieved relating to our intended or called-out mission in life.

> *"Not by might nor by power, but by My Spirit,"* says the Lord of hosts (Zechariah 4: 6). *Pursue peace with all people, and holiness, without which no one will see the Lord* (Hebrews 12: 14).

The words *Not by might* refers to our own initiative, and *nor by power* alludes to the inadequate help received from others. Connected with *but by My Spirit* satisfactorily defines the true authority that sustains Christ's Church. The words *Pursue peace and holiness without* can only occur when filled with the Holy Spirit. Man is incapable of this otherwise.

Judgment without Prejudice

Because of some Scriptures with variations, involving different times some believe that judgment will be different for those under the Old Testament law compared to today under the dispensation of grace. The answer is No! This would make God partial in His treatment of both Jew and Gentile.

The writer of Hebrews cites and Old Testament incident and is clear upon the matter. He warns the early Jewish believers about being faithful to the word of God, and not to rebel against the gospel nor convert back to Judaism like their ancestors who rebelled after leaving Egypt led by Moses.

> *Beware, brethren, lest there be in any of you an evil heart of unbelief in departing from the living God; but exhort one another daily, while it is called 'Today,' lest any of you be hardened through the deceitfulness of sin. For we have become partakers of Christ if we hold the beginning of our confidence steadfast to the end, while it is said: "Today, if you will hear His voice, Do not harden your hearts as in rebellion." For who having heard, rebelled? Indeed was it not all who came out of Egypt, led by Moses? Now with whom was He angry forth years? Was it not with those who sinned, whose corpses fell in the wilderness? And to whom did He swear that they would not enter His rest, but to those who did not obey? So we see that they could not enter in because of unbelief. Therefore, since a promise remains of entering His rest, let us fear least any of you seem to have come short of it. For indeed the gospel was preached to us as well as to them; but the word which they heard did not profit them, not being mixed with faith in those who heard it. For we who*

> *have believed do enter that rest, as He said: "So I swore in My wrath, They shall not enter My rest," although the works were finished from the foundation of the world* (Hebrews 3: 12 - 19, 4: 1 – 2).

The message is clear, the writer connects those past who once kept the law and rebelled, with these who knew better having now fallen short. He exclaims the same gospel was, preached to them as well as to us. Moses preached the gospel of the law and Jesus the gospel of grace. The writer warns, *the word which they heard did not profit them,* because they did not hold steadfast until the end.

Jesus, describing the cost of discipleship, put it in terms that the people of His day could understand, *But Jesus said to him, "No one, having put his hand to the plow, and looking back, is fit for the kingdom of God"* (Luke 9: 62).

The root cause of their rebellion was sin causing them to backslide. One un-confessed, un-repented sin will prevent us from entering His rest. This should serve as a warning to the followers of Christ, not to look back. God has completed all the provisions necessary for our salvation.

CHAPTER 8

Highway to Heaven

No U Turn

Highway of Holiness:
> *A highway shall be there, and a road, and it shall be called the Highway of Holiness. The unclean shall not pass over it, But it shall be for others. Whoever walks the road, although a fool, Shall not go astray. No lion shall be there, Nor shall any ravenous beast go up on it; It shall not be found there. But the redeemed shall walk there* (Isaiah 35: 8 – 9).

The prophet Isaiah when forth telling the coming of Jesus and His redemptive purpose compares it to a private highway. This highway as he described is to be a controlled pathway reserved only for the redeemed. The road leading to heaven a one-way single highway and all who walk on it shall be holy.

The wayfaring pilgrim's commitment required by God is within the boundary of the highway as illustrated *Whoever walks the road, although a fool, Shall not go astray.* Every provision for our redemption and our heavenly journey, have been provided, free of charge without cost. There will be no excuse accepted for not getting onboard this highway-to-heaven.

There is only one road, that will get you to heaven, and that road is Jesus Christ. Unmoved by this truth, some well-meaning misleading people including those who attend church regularly have proffered many roads lead to heaven.

The old adage you take the high road and I take the lower believing they will each eventually reach their intended destination simply does not apply. Nothing could be further from the truth.

When relating to spiritual matters humankind often seeks an easier way without cost over God's way. Jesus describes the road as being narrow and difficult not wide and broad as many would like to believe.

> *Enter by the narrow gate; for wide is the gate and broad is the way that leads to destruction, and there are many who go in by it. Because narrow is the gate and difficult is the way which leads to life, and there are few who find it* (Matthew 7: 13 – 14).

The broad way here eludes that one might try to enter heaven by a lesser means other than God's plan of salvation.

Some ill-advised advocate, being morally good and attending church is all one needs. Another misleading truth that often supports the false necessity for salvation is paved with only doing good deeds.

Many are encouraged to seek the advice of spiritualist or practice mysticism involving a variety of repetitious rituals and the list goes on. When all these avenues fail, and they will, the Bible teaches there is only one narrow road leading to heaven and that road is Jesus Christ.

Confirmation

As Christians, both young and old, we need the assurance that the road we started on will get us to our travel destination. A common anxiety that many have, when I begin this unfamiliar walk on life's highway, what road map will I use?

Long before visual voice activated GPS guidance system came into existence, our Lord promised His followers a personal guide superior to anything that man could offer.

Jesus, prior to ascending to heaven, consoled His disciples that He would not leave them alone but would send a helper or guide.

> *And I will pray the Father, and He will give you another Helper, that He may abide with you forever. However, when He the Spirit of truth, has come, He will guide you into all truth; for He will not speak on His own authority, but whatever He hears He will speak* (John 14: 16, 16: 13).

Because of this promise of help, we never have to doubt our relationship with Christ. His Spirit will always bear witness with our spirit every step of the way. The apostle Paul confirms this truth in a letter to the Romans witnessing His abiding presence. *The Spirit Himself bears witness with our spirit that we are children of God* (Romans 8: 16).

In parallel truth, John acknowledges we will know beyond doubt if we are on the correct pathway witnessed by our behavior. In the gospel of 1 John, we have a reliable comparison of right and wrong behavior expressing our true identify in the life of a person. It leaves those whom have accepted or rejected Jesus without any doubt, to where they stand in relation to Him.

> *Whoever commits sin also commits lawlessness, and sin is lawlessness. And you know that He was manifested to take away our sins, and in Him there is no sin. Whoever abides in Him does not sin. Whoever sins has neither seen Him nor know Him. Little children, let no one deceive you. He who practices righteousness is righteous, just as He is righteous. He who sins is of the devil, for the devil has sinned from the beginning. For this purpose the Son of God was manifested, that He might destroy the works of the devil. Whoever has been born of God does not sin, for His seed remains in him; and he cannot sin, because he has been born of God* (1 John 3: 4 – 9).

A brief summary of these passages indicates that one's spiritual attestation should be clear to everyone; and especially to the person involved according to their conscience in light of God's Word.

To pretend to be something that you are not is hypocritical. You cannot practice something for long that you do not possess, until the truth finds you out. Your conscience, according to the truth in you, will bear this out.

Our continual unbroken relationship with Christ will be our justification for us not to lose our spiritual standing. We have a sure promise *But if we walk in the light as He is in the light, we have fellowship with one another, and the blood of Jesus Christ His Son cleanses us from all sin* (1 John 1: 7).

The Scripture is positive confirming God's infinite mercy and grace, through Christ's blood, that is available to the believer as they walk in the light. Only in those deliberate unrepentant acts of transgressions against Christ, puts us in jeopardy of backsliding. The Holy Spirit is dependable in every situation, guesswork, is not an option!

All-encompassing Promise of Power

Holiness is the very essence of God's divine nature, and was preordained in man's creation process. This is understood in the Genesis account formed from the dust of the ground; and God breathing into his nostrils the breath of life.

In breathing His Spirit {*life*} into humankind, He fashioned him to take part of His Divine nature. In doing so, He endowed His creation with the power to live a life of holiness. Incidentally, this was lost when Adam and Eve sinned in the Garden-of-Eden through their disobedience.

The nature of holiness can only be, regained, by accepting God's plan of salvation provided in Jesus Christ. God's initial moral act of creation is re-enacted both symbolically and literally in the book of John following Jesus' death, burial, and resurrection.

Jesus commissioning His disciples said to them before departing earth to go back to heaven. *"Peace to you! As the Father has sent Me, I also send you." And when He had said this, He breathed on them, and said to them, "Receive the Holy Spirit"* (John 20: 21 – 22).

When Jesus *breathed* upon His disciples, He was confirming to them, that all power been given to Him in heaven and in earth. Moreover, reconfirmed He was the creative power present in man's first beginning, and that He is the same in our new beginning.

This literal act of breathing upon His disciples would seal the promise of the Holy Spirit prophesied by Joel 2: 28 – 29 and recorded by Luke in Acts 2: 1 – 18. This enactment similar to creation would enable them to again be a recipient of His divine nature; and would make available to them the grace needed to receive the Holy Spirit. The Holy Spirit had not come at this point, nevertheless, shall be sent upon Christ's leaving earth.

Prior to Pentecost, the Apostles were under His divine protection of grace until fulfilled on that day in the upper room provided they tarry in Jerusalem as instructed. This promise was, fulfilled as promised.

> *When the Day of Pentecost had fully come, they were all with one accord in one place. And suddenly there came a sound from heaven, as of a rushing mighty wind, and it filled the whole house where they were sitting. Then there appeared to them divided tongues, as of fire, and one sat upon each of them. And they were all filled with the Holy Spirit and began to speak with other tongues, as the Spirit gave them utterance. They were all with one accord in one place* (Acts 2: 1 – 4).

They were all present and unified concerning the promise anticipating Christ's word coming to pass. This baptism would now allow the believer a new freedom to love God with an unswerving love, glorifying Him by surrendering their selfish control and doing God's will.

Like the first Adam, man will continue to be free to make choices. Unlike a robot these choices include right and wrong, good and evil, loving God or resisting God's command if they so choose.

Incompatible Companions

After, one's conversion, there remains a conflict involving the carnal nature that exists for the duration of one being saved until sanctified. This often referred to, as the flesh, warring against the innermost desire to be spiritual minded.

Paul in his letter to the church in Galatia elaborates upon how this keeps us in bondage spiritually because of this inner conflict. He expands on this battle between the carnal mind and the spiritual minded that has that roller-coaster effect on the new convert.

> *I say then: "Walk in the Spirit, and you shall not fulfill the lust of the flesh. For the flesh lusts against the Spirit, and the Spirit against the flesh; and these are contrary to one another, so that you do not do the things that you wish"* (Galatians 5: 16 – 17).

The incompatible struggle that exists between the Spirit and flesh paralyses one's ability to live a healthy Godly life and keeps them from growing spiritually. Another example just as deadly of what Paul was writing to the Galatians are found in his letter to the church in Rome. In this letter, he addresses those who obviously believed that sin and grace are equal un-separable companions.

> *Shall we continue in sin that grace may abound? Certainly not! How shall we who died to sin live any longer in it? For the good that I will to do, I do not do; but the evil I will not to do, that I practice. For to be carnally minded is death, but to be spiritually minded is life and peace* (Romans 6: 1 - 2, 7: 19).

Sin and grace were never to be Siamese twins and by no means can be. To continue to live in sin expecting grace to unconditionally cover it is a mistake and mocks Christ's blood. We were, never meant to live on this merry-go-round.

The Apostle knew there was a proper way to live that identifies one belonging to God; in view of that, the wrong way would not be acceptable. To please God we must be free from the carnal nature that we were born with, because in our carnal state we cannot please God.

To believe carnality could co-exist in the life of the believer is ineffective and not a cure for the sin problem. The death of the carnal nature must occur.

> *Therefore do not let sin reign in your mortal body, that you should obey it in its lusts. And do not present your members as instruments of unrighteousness to sin, but present yourselves to*

> *God as being alive from the dead, and your members as instruments of righteousness to God. For sin shall not have dominion over you, for you are not under law but under grace* (Romans 6: 12 – 14).

Finally in Romans 6: 15 – 23 Paul makes the clear distinction between being a slave to sin and becoming a slave to God. The Apostle using a familiar expression involving slavery to describe holiness and its relationship one should have with God. In the context, of this passage, He instructs them to whom they obey, they are a slave to, whether a slave of sin leading to death or of obedience leading to righteousness.

They could not have it both ways and must choose as to whose slave they are, so must we. He encourages them to fully, present themselves as slaves of righteousness on the side of holiness.

Remember, the basic principle of sin bids for control of your mind and body to enslave your soul. The danger to continue on the carnal path they were on would eventually lead to their future spiritual death. Resist the devil and he will flee from you.

CHAPTER 9

Our Journey Begins

Pack your Bags

Walk Before Me:

When Abram was ninety-nine years old, the Lord appeared to Abram and said to him, "I am Almighty God; walk before Me and be blameless" (Genesis 17: 1).

Be blameless' is sometimes translated, be thou whole-hearted. The simple phrase, *Walk before Me* taken out of context could conjure up a variety of implications depending upon how you view it in relationship to your circumstances.

Some may interpret it simply to walk ahead of another person. Others may perceive it only a request out of courtesy with no significant meaning or purpose in mind. When you add the words *and be blameless,* it takes on a different importance.

With Abraham, who was ninety-nine, when God spoke those words to him could only imply one thing. He was commanding Abram to walk openly before Him to show determination with nothing to hide. This single-minded communication was a unique expression calling for obedient, endurance, and strength of character to be holy before God.

To understand the above passage God identifies Himself, as *"El shaddai"* meaning sufficient, it also means heap or dispense benefits. This conveys that God is a provider, travel companion, and guardian to those who puts their trust in Him.

When God called Abram to leave his homeland and begin his journey to a place he had never seen. He was not asking Abraham to do anything that He could not provide him with the resources to be successful. Abraham's submission to the will of God illustrates a trust in his Creator whom he had never seen.

Those same bountiful resources to be successful according to God's will are still available today. The Psalmist David as a shepherd lad portrays this truth of generosity more imaginatively when he pinned these words.

> *The Lord is my shepherd; I shall not want. Yea, though I walk through the valley of the shadow of death, I will fear no evil: You prepare a table before me in the presence of my enemies* (Psalms 23: 1, 4a, 5a).

As a shepherd, the Psalmist illustrates a relationship between the duties of the shepherd toward his sheep and the ever watchfulness of the Creator over His creation. He explains in simple terms: God as our provider, our travel companion, and our guardian.

It is God alone who made us, who can preserve us holy through Jesus Christ our Lord, as long as we are willing to follow as His sheep. Like David, we must have that same commitment and trust today. Whom we trust is the key to our success or failure.

The Journey Begins

Our earthly pilgrimage began the day we were born and will end the day we die. As in any adventure, there must be a starting point, passing of time, and a destination that concludes one's journey. I like to think my combined secular vocation and Christian experience can be both a voyage and an adventure.

The voyage because I have not yet reached my final destination; and the adventure, lies in the mystery as life unfolds. I am confident compared with most excursions there will be difficulties encountered along the way that was unforeseen, nor anticipated.

I suspect most of us can relate to a vacation or short trip when we experienced an unpleasant incident, someone got sick, or perhaps car trouble. I am often reminded that most of us are on different levels of life's' pathway and each experience is different. Each one's secular and spiritual mission may differ in time, place, and circumstances that bring us to Christ.

I am constantly learning more about the love of God and His purpose for my life daily. Regardless of biblical terms used, we all have common grounds to share when it comes to our salvation, which incidentally becomes our road map to success. Without it, we would be lost with no assurance of our future.

A New Birth

A friend once confided he could not understand what being born again means. To him the term made little sense, and he is probably not alone in understanding this biblical subtext relating to our salvation.

In the book of John, we have the story of Nicodemus a Pharisee a member of the Sanhedrin who came to Jesus by night. His visit was in pretense to inquire about the miracles Jesus had been doing. In reality wanted to know if Jesus was the prophesied Messiah; and what must he do in order to be saved.

After Jesus confirmed His identity to Nicodemus, knowing his real intention, informs him that he must be born again.

> *Jesus answered and said to him," most assuredly, I say to you, unless one is born again, he cannot see the kingdom of God." Nicodemus said to Him, "How can a man be born when he is old? Can he enter, a second time into his mother's womb and be born"*
>
> (John 3: 3 - 4)?

The term *born again* is important in understanding the gift of salvation. Just as the natural birth is essential to our earthly life, a spiritual or new birth is crucial to see the kingdom of God in our heavenly life.

Strangely enough many today, as indicated earlier, miss the importance of what Jesus was saying to Nicodemus concerning a different kind of birth.

Because Nicodemus worship rested in the law of "works," like many today, he did not have insight relating to the spiritual birth that Jesus was implying. The expression *when he is old* together with *enter a second time,* suggests that Nicodemus was getting along in age, and conveyed his feeling of defeat, helplessness and impossibility. Without doubt, some today share that same feeling. Take heart, there is hope.

Jesus knowing Nicodemus state of mind carefully explained to him what He meant.

> *Most assuredly, I say to you, "unless one is born of water and the Spirit, he cannot enter the kingdom of God. That which is born of the flesh is flesh, and that which is born of the Spirit is spirit. Do not marvel that I said to you, you must be born again"* (John 3: 5 – 7).

Our Lord's reply was simple and straightforward. His explanation cleared up the mystery for Nicodemus about the true birth Jesus was describing. He was not referring to man's physical rebirth as the ruler first thought. Jesus was speaking about a "spiritual new birth" set apart as a separate birth to man's infant birth.

Putting it another way, without the first birth one cannot live in this present world, and without the second, they cannot live in the heavenly world to come. I can relate to this because my earthly life's journey began the day I was physically born; my spiritual journey began the night I got saved from my sins and accepted Christ as my savior.

When Jesus told Nicodemus that *unless one is born of water and the Spirit* has a two-fold implication illustrated when John came baptizing with water.

> *Then Jerusalem, all Judea, and all the region around the Jordan went out to him and were baptized by him in the Jordan confessing their sins. I indeed baptize you with water unto repentance, but He who is coming after me is mightier than I, whose sandals I am not worthy to carry. He will baptize you with the Holy Spirit and fire. His winnowing fan is in His hand, and He will thoroughly clean out His threshing floor, and gather His wheat into the barn,*

> *but He will burn up the chaff with unquenchable fire*
> (Matthew 3: 5 - 6, 11 – 12).

John's baptism of water closely resembles a ceremony found in the Old Testament when a stranger came into Israel's camp and embraced the Hebrew's God. They would denounce their idols, and accept the God of Israel as their God, vowing to conform to the precepts of the law. The baptism of water by John had no saving qualities; it was in testimony of their repentance.

Like the stranger alienated from God we must denounce our sins, say yes to Christ, and obey His Word. Once saved, water baptism today is still important as a witness to what Christ has done for us. The Holy Spirit mentioned by John was reserved for the immediate future upon Jesus departing earth.

The Holy Spirit will cleanse the soul from its sin nature with fire by burning up the chaff. He is a consuming fire, and can only be experienced in His fullness, after, being saved. Our involvement in repentance and the baptism of the Holy Spirit executed by the same divine agent will become unmistakable clear.

The First Step toward God

The steps leading to salvation are not complicated, as some have tried to make it. A truth that we must all accept, no one can lay the guilt of sin upon God or anyone else, each must take full accountability for their wrongful actions.

Honesty before God and sincerity on our part are the two qualities, which is necessary before the redemptive process can ever begin. The one coming to Christ cannot be proud of their sinful past, but show remorse and humility before God with a broken and contrite spirit.

A person must first acknowledge the truth that he or she is a sinner apart from God, and is doomed unless they accept eternal life through Christ Jesus. The sincere repentant will embrace these truths in the here and now in genuine faith without regret.

> *For all have sinned and fall short of the glory of*
> *God. For the wages of sin is death; but the gift of*

God is eternal life in Christ Jesus our Lord (Romans 3: 23, 6: 23). *For godly sorrow produces repentance leading to salvation, not to be regretted; but the sorrow of the world produces death* (2 Corinthians 7: 10).

Time to Prepare our Hearts

After saved by grace, there is a period-of-time between saved and sanctified holy. In our newfound experience, we begin to leave the former life and embrace this new pathway of living. This is important in understanding what is required in making a full surrender, and is probably the most crucial time in our travel.

From the moment one is, saved, until sanctified the time table will vary depending upon the individual and their willingness to allow the Holy Spirit access to their new life.

Old things having passed away forever things are now new to the convert. Those who are infants in Christ will start behaving as a newborn individual. Paul goes on to remind them that since they are in Christ, they are to cleanse themselves perfecting holiness.

Therefore, if anyone is in Christ, he is a new creation; old things have passed away; behold, all things have become new. Therefore "Come out from among them and be separate," says the Lord. "Do not touch what is unclean, And I will receive you. I will be a Father to you, And you shall be My sons and daughters," Says the Lord Almighty. Therefore, having these promises, beloved, let us cleanse ourselves from all filthiness of the flesh and spirit, perfecting holiness in the fear of God (2 Corinthians 5: 17, 6: 17 – 18, 7: 1).

The word *Therefore,* connects what Paul wrote in the previous verses equally apply to what he is about to write. They link together to get the full meaning. We are no longer to reflect the world around us by continuing the lifestyle we previous lived or company we once kept. As we distance our self from the world, it loses its attraction to us. The farther we retreat from our sinful past the more like Christ we become.

We start to realize that we are no longer our own but belong to another. Furthermore, the more we want to be like Him the more we realize we need cleansing from our carnal nature showing His holiness. Holiness no longer becomes an option to accept or reject, but is seen as a divine requirement to gain entrance into His heavenly kingdom.

Sacrifice Required

Those, to whom Paul intended this letter were, saved, but had not, consecrated themselves to God as instruments for His service. The Apostle here is writing about a different sacrificial offering giving us the key to obtaining holiness following our conversion.

Once saved, a crucial part of our overall salvation remains to be completed comprising the requirement of a sacrifice having its roots in the Old Testament.

It is true Jesus death on the cross-abolished animal sacrifices for the last time; however, commanded here illustrates the complete voluntary submission of the participant.

> *I beseech you therefore, brethren, by the mercies of God, that you present your bodies a living sacrifice, holy, acceptable to God, which is your reasonable service. And do not be conformed to this world, but be transformed by the renewing of your mind, that you may prove what is that good and acceptable and perfect will of God* (Romans 12: 1 – 2).

Paul an intellectual Scholar in the Mosaic Law draws a parallel of Old Testament animal sacrifices ordained by God previously covered in chapter seven. This now replaced in the New Testament with a living human sacrifice. The focus now moves from the animal to the human with the exception that only a living sacrifice is accepted.

It should be, carefully noted, that the animal sacrificed in the OT was under the authority of his master and had no say in the matter.

Because we are different from the animal, given free will, we have a say in the process.

Keeping that thought in mind Jesus brings to reality an example of full submission to one's master, illustrated by His own unselfish surrender of self, denoting His death, burial, and resurrection. *And He said, "Abba, Father, all things are possible for You. Take this cup away from Me; nevertheless, not what I will, but what you will"* (Mark 14: 36b).

This reflection of His agony and obedience to become the sacrificial lamb is, witnessed in the garden prior to His crucifixion. Jesus without hesitation as a son showing His love and devotion to His Father was aware of His Father's undeniable love for Him.

We would do well to follow Christ's example of dedication and self- sacrifice and become that living sacrifice that Paul wrote about in his letter. Our death to self will be our private struggle to reach that place of full surrender to the will of God. Our, love, and devotion to God should reflect the values of Christ's love and atonement for our sins.

The Apostle demands we cannot do less and please God. His purpose and mission was never to do His will over His Father's, but always be submissive to His Father; can we do less and please our Lord? *For I have come down from heaven, not to do My own will, but the will of Him who sent Me* (John 6: 38).

No Substitute Allowed

Many today are offering up a variety of things in substitute for old fashion holy living without giving themselves fully to Christ. While striving to reach a higher standard is commendable, this disingenuous sense of worship is not new when it comes to one's unconditional devotion to God. They, often boast, of holding to a higher standard to that of the world by obeying the law and keeping a few rules.

An example of this found in the Old Testament; Malachi speaking in obedience on God's behalf warns the children of Israel against bringing a lesser sacrifice to the altar. The prophet directs his message of judgment against those whom fall careless into a false sense of security by simply going through the motions of worship without regard to whom or how they worship.

> *"A son honors his father, And a servant his master. If then I am the Father, Where is My honor? And if I am a Master, where is My reverence?" Says the Lord of hosts To you priests who despise My name. Yet you say, "In what way have we despised Your name?" "You offer defiled food on My altar, But say, In what way have we defiled You? By saying, The table of the Lord is contemptible. And when you offer the blind as a sacrifice, Is it not evil? And when you offer the lame and sick, Is it not evil? Offer it then to your governor Would he be pleased with you? Would he accept you favorably?" Says the Lord of hosts. "But cursed be the deceiver who has in his flock a male, And takes a vow, But sacrifices to the Lord what is blemished--For I am a great King," Says the Lord of hosts, "And My name is to be feared among the nations"* (Malachi 1: 6 - 8, 14).

The animals' sacrificed were blemished revealing a much deeper truth about the person's spiritual state than what appeared upon the surface. The point Malachi was making they had desecrated that which God ordained, and entered into their own substitute style of worship by offering blemished goods falsely believing they were keeping the law, only to discover different.

This must have been a great shock to them to learn that God had rejected their sacrifice. I wonder how many churches today would be shocked to learn they too have substituted the truth and were engaged in their own particular brand of worship and are empty of God's Spirit or blessings. Anything, come to mind?

Just as there is a wrong way to do things, there is a right way. The right way is always God's way. When we follow His plan for our life, life becomes more meaningful. To identify with the term *sacrifice* as a measure of acceptable worship we need to look to the Old Testament regarding animal sacrifice. In order to gain His blessings, only those animals without spot or blemish would qualify. *Your lamb shall be without blemish, a male of the first year* (Exodus 12: 5a).

These peculiarities points to Jesus Christ our high priest the final sinless sacrifice establishing His church to be holy without blemish. *That He might present her to Himself a glorious church, not having spot or wrinkle or any such thing, but that she should be holy and without blemish* (Ephesians 5: 27).

All the provisions to be a holy *without blemish* have been, provided in Christ. For that reason, holiness is attainable! Anything less than this is unacceptable before God. Our devotion should be genuine without exception, of all those who call themselves Christian.

Exemplary Example

One of the best Old Testament personifications of holiness illustrating what we have learned is, observed in the life of Abraham the founder of the Jewish Nation. To appreciate the life of Abraham and his contribution to both Judaism and our Christian heritage we need to revisit a momentous time in his life. Abraham was ninety-nine years old when the Lord appeared and said to him, *"I am Almighty God; walk before Me and be blameless"* (Genesis 17: 1b).

At this point, Abraham could not have known all that God might ask of him but was willing to trust God's judgment over his own for his future. This brings to reality that nothing is impossible to God when our determination is to be obedient; and that we are to bear fruit to be holy, as God has called us to be.

For us to fully understand and appreciate Abraham's total surrender to God and compare the similarities' of what Paul means by *present your bodies a living sacrifice* we have to look at possible the most important and challenging event in the life-of-Abraham. Abraham's obedience to walk before God was about to receive, the most crucial test known to man.

> Now it came to pass after these things that God tested Abraham, and said to him, "Abraham!" And he said, "Here I am." Then He said, "Take now

> *your son, your only son Isaac, whom you love, and go to the land of Moriah, and offer him there as a burnt offering on one of the mountains of which I shall tell you"* (Genesis 22: 1 – 2).

As the story unfolds, we see the aged patriarch who had waited so long for a rightful heir bidden to offer up his son as a burnt offering unto the Lord. The proof of a man's love for God is his willingness to obey Him without reservations with all his heart, with all of his soul, and all of his strength that is, reflected in the Shema.

In Abraham's case, his willingness to sacrifice Isaac and surrender unto God what is even dearer than his own life was the supreme test to his faith. It is little mystery why Abraham was, called "The friend of God."

According to Jewish belief, this was Abraham's tenth and greatest trial. The original Hebrew understanding is a test is, never employed for the purpose of harm, but to ascertain the power of resistance against God on the part of the one being tested. Abraham was unaware at first the instruction, *and offer him there,* was by no means an intention of accepting a human sacrifice.

According to Jewish teaching, in His command to Abraham, God did not use the word signifying the slaying of the sacrificial victim. God detested human sacrifice with an infinite abhorrence.

For the record, this story was never about Isaac {as some novelist might write}; it was always about 'Abraham' who passed the test of resistance by becoming obedient unto God; meaning Abraham had lifter the knife and was stopped from actually sacrificing Isaac.

It is very important to note; this, test, could only be made by a Divine being capable of overruling as God intervened, as was His purpose from the beginning. God required the spiritual surrender, unlike the cruel heathen deities around them who required human sacrifices.

There are several things of importance happening here to help us understand what Paul meant by *living sacrifice.* Abraham did not question God's motive for his life or, what, He was asking him to do. His obedience to God demonstrated his unconditional surrender to His will. This is a prerequisite required in sanctification to be set apart to be holy. Additional resources: *The Pentateuch & Haftorahs,* Hebrew Text English Translation & Commentary.

> **Footnote**: The Bible does not tell us what was going through Abraham's mind as he made his way to the top of the mountain. One can only speculate what he was thinking, perhaps it was back to the time when God had promised him, *In Isaac* your *seed shall be called,* (Genesis 21: 12b).
>
> In Hebrews chapter, eleven the writer gives us an insight to Abraham's faith in God even though he did not know what the outcome would be. Somewhere along his journey, he concluded that God was able to raise him from the dead.

Before we leave this chapter maybe we should ask; "What have you got in your life that you have not fully surrendered, is it money, time, a secret sin of sorts such as: alcohol, drugs, gambling, pornography, lust, anger, fear, what?" Whatever it is God has the cure. As my first pastor suggested, begin praying that God will guide you into this experience of sanctification.

CHAPTER 10

Filled With His Spirit

Full vs. Empty

Day of Pentecost:

When the Day of Pentecost had fully come, they were all with one accord in one place. And they were all filled with the Holy Spirit (Acts 2: 1, 4a).

We have covered a lot of groundwork exploring both the Old and New Testaments obligatory requirement for holiness. This chapter will address the importance of how it interrelates in the life of the believer. Let us begin with the Day of Pentecost. Peter standing alongside the eleven in Acts 2: 17 – 21 confirmed that which prophesized took place as foretold by the prophet Joel.

And it shall come to pass afterward That I will pour out My Spirit on all flesh; Your sons and your daughters shall prophecy, Your old men shall dream dreams, Your young men shall see visions. And also on My menservants and on My maidservants I will pour out My Spirit in those days. And I will show wonders in the heavens and in the earth: Blood and fire and pillars of smoke. The sun shall be turned into darkness, And the moon into blood, Before the coming of the great and awesome day of the Lord. And it shall come to pass that whosoever calls on the name of the Lord Shall be saved (Joel 2: 28 - 32a).

What is interesting Pentecost is in synchronization with the Old Testament "Feast of Weeks," traditionally known as festival of Shavuot. Both events celebrated following a special incident in history. The children of Israel observed their festival "Feast of Weeks" fifty days after their Exodus from Egypt. It occurs each year on the sixth day of the Hebrew month of Sivan commemorating the day God gave Moses the Ten Commandments on Mount Sinai, celebrating they became a nation set apart to serve God.

In similarity, today we observe Pentecost fifty days after Easter as the advent of the Holy Spirit that sets us apart to serve God. One represents a celebration of the "Law," and the other a celebration of "Grace" by which we are saved and sanctified by His cleansing power.

The Spirit of Truth

In the sixteenth chapter of John, Jesus states the future work of the Holy Spirit in the world and in the life of His followers. In preparation for this future event, in chapter seventeen, Jesus prays for Himself, His disciples, and all future believers.

> *When He, the Spirit of truth, has come, He will guide you into all truth; for He will not speak on His own authority, but whatsoever He hears He will speak; and He will tell you things to come. Sanctify them by Your truth. Your word is truth. As You sent Me into the world, I also have sent them into the world. And for their sakes I sanctify Myself, that they also may be sanctified by the truth* (John 16: 13, 17: 17 – 19).

One word that stands out over the rest is "truth" used five times. Jesus validates God's Word is true, when He prays; *Sanctify them by Your truth, Your word is truth.* It is only by truth that one can be set free; therefore, apart from God's Word remains a slave to sin.

To be set apart in the words *Sanctify them* is two-fold. The believer is to be marked for the work of ministry and to avoid all worldly desires reflecting holiness of heart, soul, and mind. Jesus seals His prayer and guarantees success by offering Himself sacrificially, purchasing theirs and our salvation by His vicarious death.

Some may question why our redemptions not completed in a single work of grace receiving all at once. I know there are some who teach and believe they obtain it all immediately or they grow into achieving holiness.

Without being judgmental, it has been an observation that those who embrace this teaching is ever striving after and never attaining. On the other hand, have witnessed many who did not know what to call it have testified to a second instantaneous work of grace. They experienced baptism with the Holy Spirit after they denounced self, surrendering their past, present, and future to God.

In truth, the problem is not with God but with man. One can never second guess, God, nor can mortal man say what God is capable or incapable of doing.

Before and After Pentecost Behavior

There is some misunderstanding concerning the disciples not belonging to Jesus prior to Pentecost. This theory does not agree with Jesus High Priestly Prayer found in John 17:6 -19. Following his prayer for Himself, Jesus testifies of giving the revelation of God to His disciples. He declares God's Word to them and confirms they received and kept His Word.

Jesus knowing that He was soon leaving this world asks the Father to keep them, as He has kept them in His Father's name, losing none except the son of perdition that the, Scripture, might be fulfilled. He asks for them by His truth to be, sanctified, which occurred on the day of Pentecost.

To best illustrate pre-Pentecostal behavior we need to look at the disciple's conduct that clearly demonstrates their carnal nature prior to receiving the Holy Spirit on the day of Pentecost. James and John the sons of Zebedee came to Jesus requesting favoritism. *Grant us that we may sit, one on Your right hand and the other on Your left, in Your glory* (Mark 10: 35 - 45 entire text not printed).

Naturally, when the other ten heard, they were greatly displeased for wanting to be exalted above their peers. Clearly, this is an example of selfishness.

Another occurrence involving James and John when Jesus was on his way to Jerusalem passing through Samaria, the village would not receive Him. The two disciples, responding out of a misguided zeal lacking knowledge of their master's cause, ask Him, *"Lord, do You want us to command fire to come down from heaven and consume them, just as Elijah did"* (Luke 9: 51-56 entire text not printed).

Their inappropriate behavior, causes Jesus to rebuke them for wanting to call down fire and destroy them as Elijah had done, recorded in 2 Kings 1: 10 – 12. This should serve as a warning to all of us to avoid a superior religious zeal and not to assume something until proven or act irrationally without all the facts. We must remember vengeance belongs to God.

On separate occasions the apostle Peter, one of the inner circle, succumbed to his fleshly nature. Before Pentecost, he was impetuous, hotheaded, reckless, impulsive, and cowardly, seldom considering the outcome of his actions. A case in point in Mark 8: 31 – 33, Jesus using this opportunity was teaching His disciples concerning His death when Peter took Him aside and began to rebuke the Lord.

Because of the serious nature of Peter's outburst Jesus reprimanded him for not being mindful of the things of God, but of men. Jesus was not calling Peter Satan and was only pointing out his disapproval concerning His death being an obstacle and offense as if Satan had said it himself.

A similar case in point recorded in John 13: 36 – 38, Peter boasts that he would lay down his life for our Lord only to deny Him three times as Jesus foretold he would. Peter though meaning well with best intentions, was one who speaks before they think. What Peter wanted to do he lacked the power to do, as witnessed in his life before being, filled with the Holy Spirit.

In opposite following Pentecost, Peter, James and John, and the others filled with the Holy Spirit, became different persons. Peter was now courageous, self-assured, self-confident, influential, and persuasive to the end of his life. This new spirit, including his peers, was now determined to do what God willed, and possessed the power through Christ to carry it to completion.

After Pentecost, Peter standing up with the apostles preached a bold sermon and three thousand converted that day. He later healed a lame man and again used the opportunity to preach the gospel with boldness. Later Peter and John Acts 2: - 4: arrested and forbidden to speak or teach in Jesus name, naturally, they did not obey.

Besides the apostle Paul, Peter became one of the most prominent of the apostles. The list goes on containing other courageous deeds recorded in acts about their obedience and valor resulting in martyrdom.

Sanctification a Second Work of Grace

It is impossible for the sinner to know the depth of his sin problem when he first comes to Christ. God in His full redemption process accommodates man according to his ability to understand complex revelations, and receive God's grace as his faith allows.

The only thing he knows for, certain, is that he has transgressed against God, and needs forgiveness for the sins he has committed. He is not aware nor does he know that he needs cleansing from his carnal nature until later.

Sanctification is not the end; it is the means to an end. This is not to imply that after one has been, filled with the Holy Spirit, their spiritual growth stops or they never need future anointing of the Holy Spirit.

Just the opposite occurs, one grows in His grace and knowledge daily as God reveals His will to them. His Word clearly teaches that God does justify and sanctify the believer in two distinct functions of grace embodied in one designed plan of salvation.

> *Now when the apostles who were at Jerusalem heard that Samaria had received the word of God, they sent Peter and John to them, who, when they had come down prayed for them that they might receive the Holy Spirit. For as yet He had fallen upon none of them. They had only been baptized in the name of the Lord Jesus. Then they laid hands on them, and they received the Holy Spirit* (Acts 8: 14 – 17). *And it happened, while Apollos was at Corinth, that Paul, having passed through the upper regions, came to Ephesus. And finding some disciples he said*

> *to them, "Did you receive the Holy Spirit when you believed?" So they said to him, "We have not so much as heard whether there is a Holy Spirit." And he said to them, "Into what then were you baptized?" So they said, "Into John's baptism." Then Paul said, "John indeed baptized with a baptism of repentance, saying to the people that they should believe on Him who would come after him, that is, on Christ Jesus." When they heard this, they were baptized in the name of the Lord Jesus. And when Paul had laid hands on them, the Holy Spirit came upon them, and they spoke with tongues and prophesied* (Acts 19: 1 – 6).

Both accounts give us a perfect example of what took place following initially believing and after accepting Christ as their savior. Depicted in Paul's own conversion documented by Luke, in the book of Acts, is one of the clearest complete chronological accounts of two separate works of grace.

Paul was on his way to Damascus to bring back to Jerusalem those who were followers of Christ when something unexpected occurred.

> *Then Saul, still breathing threats and murder against the disciples of the Lord, went to the high priest and asked letters from him to the synagogues of Damascus, so that if he found any who were of the Way whether men or women, he might bring them bound to Jerusalem. As he journeyed he came near Damascus, and suddenly a light shone around him from heaven. Then he fell to the ground, and heard a voice saying to him, "Saul, Saul, why are you persecuting Me?" And he said, "Who are you Lord?" Then the Lord said, "I am Jesus, whom you are persecuting. It is hard for you to kick against the goads." So he, trembling and astonished, said, "Lord what do you want me to do?" Then the Lord*

> said, "Arise and go into the city, and you will be told what you must do." Now there was a certain disciple at Damascus named Ananias; and to him the Lord said in a vision, "Ananias." And he said, "Here I am, Lord." So the Lord said to him, "Arise and go to the street called Straight, and inquire at the house of Judas for one called Saul of Tarsus, for behold, he is praying. And in a vision he has seen a man named Ananias coming in and putting his hand on him, so that he might receive his sight." Then Ananias answered, "Lord I have heard from many about this man, how much harm he has done to Your saints in Jerusalem. And here he has authority from the chief priests to bind all who call on Your name." But the Lord said to him, "Go for he is a chosen vessel of Mine to bear My name before Gentiles, kings, and the children of Israel. For I will show him how many things he must suffer for My name's sake." And Ananias went his way and entered the house; and laying his hand on him he said, "Brother Saul, the Lord Jesus, who appeared to you on the road as you came, has sent me that you may receive your sight and be filled with the Holy Spirit" (Acts 9: 1 – 6, 10 – 17).

Later Luke gives a summary account of Paul's conversion to King Agrippa; and in verse-eighteen recounts his earthly mission to the lost, which included preaching forgiveness of sin and sanctification by faith.

> *To open their eyes, in order to turn from darkness to light, and from the power of Satan to God, that they may receive forgiveness of sins and an inheritance among those who are sanctified by faith in Me* (Acts 26: 12 – 18 entire text not printed).

When seeking the truth these two distinct accounts of grace should suffice: (1) receiving forgiveness of sins, and (2) sanctified by faith (filled with the Holy Spirit) is difficult to deny.

To summarize after coming to Christ, we soon begin to realize we belong to another and our life now embraces a different purpose causing one to surrender daily to a higher power. The battle to do God's, will and remain holy does not stop after ones sanctified as the Apostle Paul understood.

In his letter to the Corinthians, Paul alludes that his life is lived as the life of a martyr constantly exposed to death bringing with him those in Christ. The apostle learned early the importance of daily surrender, as should we, before a life can truly flourish as God intended. *I affirm, by the boasting in you which I have in Christ Jesus our Lord, I die daily* (1 Corinthians 15: 31).

Like the early disciples, our consecration is a daily spiritual death to self if we are to be good stewards and bear much fruit otherwise our life will be barren. Our success cannot occur outside of God's grace.

The disciples were the first to learn this truth when Jesus spoke about this to His Apostles in reference to His own death and resurrection reflected in the grain of wheat.

> *Most assuredly, I say to you, "unless a grain of wheat falls into the ground and dies, it remains alone; but if it dies, it produces much grain. He who loves his life will lose it, and he who hates his life in this world will keep it for eternal life. If anyone serves Me, let him follow Me; and where I am, there My servant will be also. If anyone serves Me, him My Father will honor"* (John 12: 24 – 26).

The illustration comparing His death to a grain of wheat fulfills the way to redeem a lost world that by His death and resurrection we may live, and all those who follow Him. The warning to His disciples and all of us must be willing to lose our life if necessary. The way to heaven is through self-denial reflecting our total surrender to our Lord.

The Greatest Example

The greatest example of selfless devotion was in the life of Christ observed in the Garden-of-Gethsemane prior to Him going to the cross. After Jesus, celebrating the Passover with His disciples knowing what was in His immediate future they all sung a hymn and went out to the Mount of Olives to pray. There in His most sacrificial circumstance gives us the greatest example of surrendering to the will of God.

> *Then Jesus came with them to a place called Gethsemane, and said to the Disciples, "Sit here while I go and pray over there." And He took with Him Peter and the two sons of Zebedee, and He began to be sorrowful and deeply distressed. Then He said to them, "My soul is exceedingly sorrowful, even to death. Stay here and watch with Me." He went a little further and fell on His face, and prayed saying, "O My father, if it is possible, let this cup pass from Me; nevertheless, not as I will, but as You will"* (Matthew 26: 36 – 39).

You cannot experience all of God until first God has all one hundred percent of you. Anything less is not acceptable. In reality there is no such thing as an "Ivory soap" Christian where ninety-nine/forty-four one hundred percent pure is good enough.

I like the slogan because it speaks well for the product it represents and the buyer knows what to expect from it. In parallel the depth of our devotion, not as I will, *but to do His will*, observed in his or her daily activity is crucial.

Bondservant Forever

In the New Testament, the label bondservant identifies several of the disciples and their relationship to Jesus. No doubt, they borrowed the title from the book of Exodus that offers a description of a slave or servant and their obligation to their master Exodus 21: 1 – 6. Conceivably this is where Paul, Timothy, Jude, Peter, and James got their inspiration to call themselves a bondservant of Christ seeing they were schooled in the Torah.

A review of their characteristics involving the indebtedness to their master is of vital importance in understanding our relationship to Christ. In the Old Testament, the bondservant served for six years and released in the seventh year of his service called the year of Jubilee. If the servant came to the master by himself, then he was free to leave by himself. Likewise, if he came in with a wife he was free to leave with his wife.

In dissimilar circumstances, if his master provided him a wife then he was not free to leave with her or any children they might have during his time of service. They became his master's property.

However, if the servant at the time of Jubilee plainly says, *"I love my master, my wife, and my children; I will not go out free"* (Exodus 21: 5). What is interesting and very important note the order of his love and devotion, first to his master, then his wife, and last his children.

Once the servant makes the key decision, *I will not go out free* the master brings him to the judges as a witness of his own free will offers himself to his master for life.

The master then brings him to his door and with an awl pierces a hole in his ear, a mark of ownership. According to Jewish accepted belief, the piercing of the ear at the doorpost symbolizes the attachment of the slave to his master's household forever. This is imperative in appreciating a bondservant and the price he pays for the privilege of serving his master.

I see a parallel to the servant and his master in our relationship to Christ, who said, *"He who loves father or mother more than me is not worthy of Me"* (Matthew 10: 37a). Jesus never implies that one should not love his or her family. It does suggest that one's priority is important.

Unfortunate some have had to make that choice because there no longer accepted in their home after coming to Christ. The Bible is clear on this.

To summarize, Paul and the other disciples who call themselves bondservants to Christ are comparable to the servant in the Old Testament, bearing similar qualities, a servant forever of their own free will by the grace of God. The servant's obligation to his master was greater that the sense of duty to his wife and children because he owed everything to his master, who in return provides all of his provisions care and protection.

In serving his master faithfully, he was insuring the wellbeing of his family. It only makes sense if an earthly master does that for his servant how much more will Christ provide for those who love and serve Him. Can we be less holy and please our Lord?

Personal Testimony

In sharing my testimony to God's unending grace in hope that it will help someone who may be struggling in his or her own life concerning the experience of holiness. As mentioned earlier one's experience may differ in time, place, and circumstances while the end, results, can be the same.

My early childhood was relatively average for the day-and-age I grew up in coming from a non-Christian home and only attended Sunday school infrequently.

As far as the Bible is concerned, I considered myself naive to even its basic teaching and did not have preconceived ideas about one's salvation. This eliminated biased hurdles to overcome in search for deliverance. Fortunate for me there was a pastor's influence in my early days I never forgot who was instrumental in my coming to Christ.

The thing that stood out most about this man of God, he was at peace with himself and God. I recall wanting to have this same peace one day; and my thoughts were, "If I ever get religion I want the kind reverend Cooper has." Beyond that, I knew very little about Christianity.

I managed to make it through high school in June 1954, the age of seventeen. The long awaited graduation day had finally arrived. Like most high school graduates, the spirit of excitement was high, what a thrill, and look out future here I come. I was eagerly standing on the threshold of opportunity, so I thought. We all have our dreams, and later the Statler Brothers captured it all in their song "The class of 57" which I enjoy to this day.

After joining the military and serving in two branches of our Armed Forces, life was going nowhere. Following my discharge, in the course of my search for peace with my Creator, I attended several different churches. One of those churches I was acquainted with earlier was the Church of the Nazarene, a holiness Church.

In my youth, a young Nazarene pastor whom aforementioned had made an impact upon my life I never forgot. This pastor had prayed for me over the years that God would keep His hand upon me and bring me into a saving relationship with Jesus Christ. Looking back upon life, I can see how God answered his prayers for my safety more than once. His prayers for my salvation was about to be answered.

On April 29, 1962, in the evening service, pastor Blackmon delivered a wonderful message and there was a beautiful spirit that permeated the service. Standing at the crossroads of life; weighing a decision to accept Christ, facing a past to be forgiven never again remembered against me, or I could continue as before with a future with no hope or certainty.

I could no longer run or push God aside. I had to face my sin and guilt. Under conviction in the closing moments of the service, I asked "God to forgive me of my sins" and accepted Christ as my savior. As the Bible promises, became a new creature in Christ.

In the pastors Sunday school class, following my conversion, he began to encourage the class to seek sanctification. I began to seek in prayer for the experience in something I did not understand. It was those moment-by-moment times in prayer, between regeneration (saved) and consecration, that I felt the grace of God drawing me closer to a full commitment.

The pastor's sermon that morning was about totally surrendering to the will of God. This time conviction was different from the past. My guilt was not about any sins that I had committed. The persuasion this time was the need to turn everything over to Christ without reservation. On June 6, 1962, God answered that prayer. The old man that carnal nature died to self that morning, and the Lord sanctified me holy.

For the first time, I experienced in and through Christ, the true meaning of *love, joy, and peace* (Galatians 5: 22 entire text not printed). I later learned these were some of the evidence of the fruit of the Spirit. Because of the transformation in my life, my *Bread of Tears* became my "Bread of Life" and for the first time I was free.

Victory in Jesus

You want victory, genuine victory, then you must do as Jesus taught, come and put everything upon the altar of God withholding nothing including yourself so God may fill you with His Holy Spirit. When you fully consecrate yourself, God will do the rest as Paul instructed the church.

> *Abstain from every form of evil. Now may the God of peace Himself sanctify you completely; and may your whole spirit, soul, and body be preserved blameless at the coming of our Lord Jesus Christ. He who calls you is faithful, who also will do it* (1 Thessalonians 5: 22 – 24).

The process of holiness begins in regeneration when one repents coming to Christ confessing their sins. A second work of grace, our sanctification, occurs when we fully yield ourselves to God without reservations. Cleansing is God's work in purifying the heart from its carnal nature. God can only sanctify the believer filling them with the Holy Spirit after they consecrate themselves.

To help explain complete salvation or holiness, using this comparison illustrates one's sin nature compared with that of a tree. A tree normally described as consisting of roots, a trunk, and supporting branches adorned with leaves. The trees trunk, including roots, symbolizes the carnal nature one is born with. The branches relate to the sins committed in life.

Have you ever watched a tree removal service remove a tree? The removal of the tree is a two-step procedure, first the branches pruned from the tree, then the stump removed by a separate action utilizing the same cutting process.

In similar terms, after the Holy Spirit has completed its trimming of sin branches (involving repentance) the carnal stump remains until successfully removed (consecration/sanctification). An important truth that we cannot take lightly; if the stump is not removed, within a short time after we are initially saved, it will begin to sprout limbs again.

Remember Paul said that the carnal mind is not subject to the law of God. The removal of the carnal nature is of the utmost importance to live victorious in Christ. In his first letter to the Corinthians 3:1 – 4, Paul admonished the believers as being babes in Christ who were continuing to act out of their carnal state. He accused them of acting like mere men, not spiritual minded, similar to the way Peter acted when he rebuked Jesus. Their spiritual condition was that of envy, strife, and divisions among them.

This may explain why so many people struggle with their addictions following their conversion; they fail to complete the process of full surrender. What do you have to lose?

CHAPTER 11

Our Final Destination

Finally Home

Heaven or Hell:

> *His Lord said to him, "Well done, good and faithful servant; you have been faithful over a few things, I will make you ruler over many things. Enter into the joy of your Lord. Cast the unprofitable servant into outer darkness. There will be weeping and gnashing of teeth"* (Matthew 25: 23, 30).

It is much easier to believe in a loving God who does not punish rather than a just God who would condemn someone to hell. These words of our Lord's account describe the faithful and the unfaithful servant implicating their destiny determining their final abode throughout eternity. This contrast should leave no doubt that a person will dwell in one of two places.

If you have ever had misgivings concerning eternity, Jesus dispels all doubts using the parable of talents to describe an absolute infinite truth. He commends the faithful and condemns the unfaithful in the same portion of Scripture. God set the standard this is why salvation is so important. The truth is no one has to go there because in His love and mercy God provides a way of escape.

Heaven

Heaven revealed in the Bible portrayed in several ways as a tangible inhabitable place. One, it is pictured a separate location apart from the earth as a division of the universe in God's creation process Genesis 1: 1. Abram declared that God is the possessor of both heaven and earth Genesis 14: 19, 22. What God possesses He can control who enters and those not allowed to enter His kingdom.

Jesus invites His followers to lay up their treasures in heaven where they will never be, destroyed. This invite should instill a sense of inheritance and make us feel a part of belonging Matthew 6: 19 – 21.

In the book of Revelations *Then I, John, saw the holy city, New Jerusalem, coming down out of heaven from God, prepared as a bride adorned for her husband* (Revelations 21: 2). He goes on to describe the location as a place where there are no sorrow, no crying, no pain, and no more death.

In his description, he portrays the city as a scene of untold beauty. John uses precious stones to describe the walls of the city and tells of the streets of pure gold. He closes the chapter with a sobering truth concerning the inhabitants identified as, *only those who are written in the 'Lamb's Book of Life* (Revelations 21: 27).

A person can miss many things in this life; they do not want to miss heaven. This is where all the redeemed will be with Jesus throughout eternity. Heaven is the only real thing that matters in this life. We have only this lifetime to prepare for eternity to come. Paul wrote, *But as it is written: Eye has not seen, nor ear heard, Nor have entered into the heart of man The things which God has prepared for those who love Him* (1 Corinthians 2: 9). To miss heaven is to miss everything.

Hell

The Bible describes hell opposite of heaven, a place of weeping, gnashing of teeth, unquenchable fire, torment, outer darkness, and everlasting punishment to mention a few. In fact, it is so real the New Testament mentions it using a variety of ways. Here are only fifty-four references:

The word hell thirteen times; Torment ten times, five of those in Revelation; Hades eleven times, four in Revelation; Fire and Brimstone seven times, six in Revelation; Flame six times, three in Revelation, and gnashing of teeth seven times.

As you can see, there are numerous references to hell in the Bible. Jesus spoke more on the subject than any other single topic, is it any wonder? Hell is a one-way ticket from everlasting to everlasting!

Who is Responsible?

The Psalmist David once asked, *What is man that You are mindful of him, And the son of man that You visit him* (Psalms 8: 4)? He went on to answer his own question by describing man as being made a little lower than the angels being crowned with glory and honor. This unique creation placed man in a one of its kind category.

Let us examine the facts; man created separate from the animals; gifted like His Creator possessing moral character, immortality, and freedom of will. Created with the ability to make decisions and take responsibility verified in man having dominion over the animals. This truth mirrors in the care of the sheep, oxen, beasts of the field, birds of the air, and the fish of the sea.

Therefore, man alone is responsible for his own actions which is very important in understanding what I' am about to write and difficult to explain. How can a loving God see one of His creations perish in hell? Having asked, no doubt is an inquiry that many cannot find any answer that satisfies their search for the truth.

This in itself is a very difficult question, therefore many offer theories of those saved and who, if any, will be lost. The answer is in God's sovereign spiritual (holy) relationship to His creation when you consider the following.

God is eternal and was present before anything that now appears John 1: 1 – 3. Prior to creation God was self-sufficient and had no need of anything for his joy, comfort, or pleasure. God is not a part of His creation in any form, as some believe. If a tree is, consumed, in a forest fire does not mean that a small part of God burned up with the tree.

Just the opposite is true; all creation is subject to Him. Categorically then God was before creation, was present in all creation, and always will be present.

As a final point, God's not related to man in the same way we are with humankind. God does not have the same connection to us as we have to one another in our physical makeup. Man formed from the dust of the ground and made a living being. God has no, connection to dust as being a part of, or coming from.

All of Adams offspring possesses a physical biological relationship. Our association to God is spiritual rather than physical, established upon a loving obedient moral relationship reflecting God's holiness that cannot tolerate sin. Our spirit is the only thing that will live throughout eternity.

Back to our question, how can a loving God allow one of his creations to perish in hell? This is difficult to accept when measured alongside as parents we love our children and often say that we would give our life for our children. I do not doubt that you would do this.

God's love, though there is no biological connection, far exceeds any parents love. God has provided for your salvation by the death of His only begotten Son who sacrificially shed His blood for you when you could not save yourself.

You see God cannot rescue you against your will, if you determine not to repent and accept Christ as your savior you leave God no choice. As hard as we try we cannot fathom what God did for us and how great a price He paid for our redemption.

No earthly love will ever match His never dying love. Our Lord's death for our sins shows the love and length of mercy that God extended to keep us out of a devil's hell that we all deserved. God is innocent and blameless in one being eternally lost.

Your sentence of hell cannot be, attributed, to anything God has done. The guilt is yours because you made it impossible for God to save you if you do not repent and accept Christ. This being true whom then ultimately is responsible for someone going there. You are!

The Finality of Hell

When you think of something as final what comes to mind, it is over, finished, no chance of reoccurrence. While many of us may accept what has occurred as final, the outcome irrevocable, others do not share this same view. This kind of thinking leads into my next statement where some believe hell is only temporary.

They believe it's' only a place of purification where one goes to heaven after a short time. Jesus does not suggest this possibility in his story of the rich man and Lazarus found in Luke 16: 19 – 31. Jesus defines a great gulf that is fixed, and will not allow passage from hell to heaven or the reverse.

He validates this truth relating to the rich man in hell who wanted Lazarus to dip the tip of his finger in water and cool his tongue. Then he begs Abraham to send Lazarus to go and warn his five brothers so they could escape the same punishment, neither occurred.

When mining for truth you can count on, we should turn to Scripture, God's infallible word. In this example, Solomon uses an understandable illustration proven by actual events that no one can deny. *If the clouds are full of rain, They empty themselves upon the earth; And if a tree falls to the South or the North, In the place where the tree falls, there it shall lie* (Ecclesiastes 11: 3).

Everyone can testify certain as the clouds are full of rain, they will empty their drops upon the earth; you can count on it happening. Equally undeniable, a tree that fall North or South will lie where it fell. This illustrates in whatever state the body dies saved or lost, explained by the direction the tree falls, will be the same in the world everlasting.

In Revelations John makes the distinction very clear about the finality of both places and who goes there. Jesus makes it clear to John after the final judgment those names not found in the *Book of Life are cast into the lake of fire* (Revelations 20). Only those found written in the *Lamb's Book of Life* go to heaven (Revelations 21). Jesus warns that He is coming quickly and reemphasizes who will be, allowed in, and who will be, left outside Revelations 22.

Afterward though difficult to accept, there is no mention of Christ ever visiting hell or having anything to do with those who are there. Just as God is able to forget the sins of those who confess them before Him and accepts Christ, He will forget those in hell. They are doomed to everlasting punishment. God is not going to lament over those who go to hell throughout eternity.

For those who are still uncertain concerning the finality of punishment, one last truth to consider. There is never a mention of the names of those in hell as those in heaven Revelations 20: 13 – 15. Just as the rich man remained nameless in Jesus' parable, only their deeds recorded in a book remembered, unlike those whose names found in the *Book of Life*.

Their sinful deeds recorded in the book will continue to condemn him or her for eternity. They will be alone in their torment and pain for eternity without mercy away from God and God's people. All their anguish and cries even their being sorry, will not relinquish what they are suffering.

Most ministers today avoid preaching on the subject of hell because they do not wish to upset people. We have but one life to get things right not as the reincarnate believe. They believe they can continue to come back in some life form until they get it right.

The death rate is 100 percent; there is no better time than right now to repent and ask Christ to come into your heart. My prayer for you is that you want put off your salvation reflecting holiness. Afterward share this gospel with your friends that they too might receive Jesus and escape eternal punishment. This is the greatest gift you will ever receive or give to another.

In closing, Jesus would never tell such a story of the rich man and Lazarus if it were not true. Think about the last time you burned yourself, a small cut or scrape. What was the pain like, was it a few minutes, an hour, or even a day or more. Consider for a moment, how long eternity will be in comparison. You do not want to go there! Can we do less than to warn those who are lost? Remember, *as it is appointed for men to die once, but after this the judgment* (Hebrews 9: 27).

Repent! Repent! Repent!

CHAPTER 12

Redemption

Debt Paid

Call to Repentance:
The Lord is not slack concerning His promise, as some count slackness, but is longsuffering toward us, not willing that any should perish but that all should come to repentance (2 Peter 3: 9).

Everyone called to repentance begs the question, who will answer the call. This bonus chapter is a cohesive explanation of humankinds search for redemption combined with some of the truths we have already incorporated in unison with this study. This review offers a no-nonsense look at deliverance from another approach as it applies to humanity.

In both Psalms and Hebrews, introduces the question *What is man that you are mindful of him* (Psalms 8: 4a, Hebrews 2: 6a)? The human race since the beginning of existence upon earth, no doubt has thought about these things. Scholars and nonprofessionals alike have been trying to answer that question for centuries.

In an attempt to answer *what is man,* several schools of thought have shaped our modern day society comprising some of our values both good and bad. Based upon man's self-discovery, some are without merit perpetuated as an easy way out.

This is not to imply some do not have value in educating societies in their quest for truth. These influences usually founded in one's social order often changes according to so-called greater findings of truth.

Many of these changes are determinable to society when promoted outside biblical truth. These various schools of thought often leave the human race with more questions in their search for satisfactory answers. A brief definition follows:

Schools of Thought

Sociology – A science pertaining to our society as an organized body within its social structure studying the development of organized human behavior. Exploring carefully both individuals, and to the same degree groups within the society. Their focus includes but not limited to economics, race, gender, culture, sexuality, and religion discovering the sequence each play in making up the society.

Anthropology - Historically differs from Sociology, it sees man in his own culture using all its pieces such as race, physical makeup, environment, and social relations using a comparative approach to obtain its conclusion of truth concerning one's habit. Anthropology is a cross- cultural study of humankind. In the United States, it encompasses four fields of study: cultural, archeological, linguistic, and biological.

Psychology - Relates to the world in which we live understanding how people learn, think, feel, and act in society. It focuses more on the mental order rather than physical behavior of people.

Philosophy - Is the branch of knowledge used to understand the world in which we live. It employs abstract principles based upon theories that are intellectually possible rather than anything specific or concrete. Its search for truth employs logical reasoning rather than actual or factual observations.

Theology - A study of our Christian faith establishing one's belief about God in creation, humankind's existence upon earth, where they came from, their purpose upon earth, and where they are bound for. Only the Bible contains absolute truths concerning the true nature of humanity connecting where man came from, why he is here, and where he is going.

There is little doubt why people are confused about themselves when there is so little agreement among many scholars including religious schools of thought.   The liberation or redemption of humankind is not an easy subject to write about especially when so many scholars have different interpretations upon the subject matter pertaining to the Bible.

Biblical truth in its message without being "spiritually discerned" approaching with faith cannot be comprehended. Paul's letter to the Church of Corinth teaches the natural unregenerate man is incapable of discerning this truth. To the natural man the things of God are foolishness to him, which he cannot comprehend or embrace. *... the natural man does not receive the things of the Spirit of God, for they are foolishness to him; nor can he know them, because they are spiritually discerned* (1 Corinthians 2: 14). Therefore, a change must first occur before anyone can have an appreciation for the truth of God.

Bankrupt without Hope Until

Men and women have been struggling with their identity since the beginning of time. They failed to take into account that humanity was living in a fallen state incapable of fully understanding or rescuing himself. In their search, they tried to reinvent themselves using these various schools of thought. When their human efforts were botched, they failed to see the real problem that was staring them in the face.

There was a need for a higher truth outside of man's autonomous self-discovery. Here we depart from the major secular schools of thought and focus on what the Bible offers in our search for truth. When Adam and Eve disobeyed God in the Garden-of-Eden sin entered the human race making Adam the natural or carnal man causing mayhem ever since.

Sin placed man in a category all by himself. As the result of their sinful nature, they were incapable of delivering themselves from the evil that separated them from God's highest blessing, mainly fellowship with their Heavenly Father.

In order to restore a relationship with God a redeemer must be, provided, and no one on earth could provide this. Here we have the first promise of God's plan of salvation. *And I will put enmity between you and the woman, and between your seed and her seed; He shall bruise your head, and you shall bruise His heel* (Genesis 3: 15).

This passage is referring to the coming of Jesus Christ. Jesus according to God's plan will be born of a virgin, thus bruising the head of the serpent. The bruising of His heel refers to our Lord's death providing for the salvation for all humankind. Here we see God choosing His only begotten Son a sacrifice for our redemption. God is the only one merciful and loving enough to do this for us as sinners. Christ, *"was and is"* the only one worthy enough to pay this price.

Yet many refuse His gift in search of something else as many are doing today. The sad truth there is no other way; the good news, Christ is the only way to God and forgiveness. No substitute allowed.

What Is a Soul Worth

To salvage something whatever the object, usually carries with it the belief the damaged merchandise can be, restored! Satisfactory restoration of a priceless object can only be, accomplished by a knowledgeable skilled artisan. When using the terms "to redeem or to salvage" usually implies the same principles used describing the restoration process. When something is worth saving, it is usually worth redeeming regardless the cost.

To put this in our modern day economy the cost for our redemption is greater than the sum total of the world and all its inhabitants, past, present, and future. No human can calculate the cost, only God can do this. Jesus said, *"For what profit is it to a man if he gains the whole world, and loses his own soul? Or what will a man give in exchange for his soul"* (Matthew 16: 26)?

Simply stated, man was bankrupt; they had nothing to bargain with even if he owned the world he could not buy back his salvation. If the human race was to become rescued, or redeemed someone else had to take the initiative and provide the means outside of man's ability.

Putting this in perspective, have you ever bought something that was precious to you? Perhaps most of us have at one time or another.

How did you feel afterward? No doubt, you felt a sense of pride to have it no matter the cost you believed that it was worth every dollar you paid for it. Would you feel differently should it become, damaged, no fault of yours? Although inadequate, this is the same concept used in the New Testament that describes our salvation. A loving and caring God, through no fault of His, bought our deliverance for a price; a price that no man could afford.

A Reality Checkup

By now you may be thinking, are we not all Christians? We are civilized; we observe holy days; we promote a national day of prayer; we even have "In God We Trust" on our money. Surely, this must make us a Christian perpetuated by society and offered to establish its worth.

As catchwords, there is value in what they represent. When this becomes a pretense or substitute to following God's plan for moral living, then this becomes extremely dangerous.

> *Hear, O heavens, and give ear, O earth! For the Lord has spoken: "I have nourished and brought up children, and they have rebelled against Me. The ox knows its owner, and the donkey its master's crib; But Israel does not know, My people do not consider. Alas sinful nation, A people laden with iniquity, a brood of evildoers, Children who are corrupters! They have forsaken the Lord, They have provoked to anger The Holy One of Israel, They have turned away backward. Hear the word of the Lord, You rulers of Sodom; Give ear to the law of our God, You people of Gomorrah: To what purpose is the multitude of your sacrifices to Me?" Says the Lord. "I have had enough of burnt offerings of rams, and the fat of fed cattle. I do not delight in the blood of bulls, or of lambs, or goats. When ye come to appear before Me, who has required this from*

your hand, to trample my courts? Bring no more futile sacrifices; Incense is an abomination to Me. The new Moons, the Sabbaths, and the calling of assemblies, I cannot endure iniquity and the sacred meeting. Your New Moons and your appointed feasts My soul hates; They are a trouble to Me, I am weary of bearing them. When you spread out your hands, I will hide My eyes from you; Even though you make many prayers, I will not hear. Your hands are full of blood. Wash yourselves, make yourselves clean; Put away the evil of your doings from before My eyes. Cease to do evil, Learn to do good; Seek justice, Rebuke the oppressor, Defend the fatherless, Plead for the widow. Come now let us reason together," says the Lord, *"Though your sins are like scarlet, they shall be as white as snow; Though they are red like crimson, they shall be as wool. If you are willing and obedient, you shall eat the good of the land; But if ye refuse and rebel, you shall be devoured by the sword; for the mouth of the Lord has spoken"* (Isaiah 1: 2 - 4, 10 – 20). *Now we know that God does not hear sinners; but if anyone is a worshiper of God and does His will, He hears him* (John 9: 31).

Counterfeit worship produces false results. To go through insincere motions does not automatically invoke God's blessings as Isaiah points out. The expression, *You rulers of Sodom and You people of Gomorrah* does not mean that Isaiah's message was for the two cities of the plains. He was merely using them to describe Israel's conduct.

The significance of this truth is that God cannot be, fooled. He knows who belongs to Him and who is only pretending. The pretenders should never presume that God hears them unless their prayer is a prayer of repentance understood in *God does not hear sinners.*

The prophet points out that even the most elaborate form of worship unaccompanied by righteous conduct is hypocritical, and this type of false worship would bring about God's wrath. Their worship was superficial and without meaning. They were doing what God's Word describes as, *having a form of godliness but denying its power* (2 Timothy 3: 5a).

Nauseated by their false behavior, God declares that even the ox and donkey are smarter. At least the ox and donkey knows who their owners are and who keeps them. I wonder if we in 'America' are as smart at times. Do you see any resemblance of this today?

Open My Eyes

Our souls are serious business; there is no business in life more valuable. Open my eyes Lord that I might see should be the prayer on every ones lips. One should never take God's offer of salvation lightly without contemplating the outcome.

We are here upon this earth for a limited amount of time. The choice we make about our redemption before we die is crucial concerning where you will spend eternity. *And as it is appointed for men to die once, but after this the judgment* (Hebrews 9: 27).

Notice the writer uses the word *once,* a sound warning to everyone, this is very important. Despite some popular opinion of reincarnation, believing we will get one chance after another until we get it right is pure rubbish. To the contrary only sincere repentance guarantees God's favor. There are no other options in life nor has its equal.

The Apostle Paul, in his second letter to the Thessalonians gives this warning about the end times and evil seducing spirits.

> *Let no one deceive you by any means; for that Day will not come unless the falling away comes first, and the man of sin is revealed, the son of perdition. The coming of the lawless one is according to the*

> *working of Satan, with all power, signs, and lying wonders, and with all unrighteous deception among those who perish, because they did not receive the love of the truth, that they might be saved. And for this reason God will send them strong delusions, that they should believe the lie, that they all may be condemned who did not believe the truth but had pleasure in unrighteousness* (2 Thessalonians 2: 3, 9 – 12).

Because of man's unrighteousness and disrespect for truth, God will permit false impressions to occupy their mind. Whereby, it becomes easier to believe a lie rather than the truth especially when the lie becomes the truth to them. This puts in motion to prefer false teaching above the gospel message of rescue.

A pattern to this degree makes it easier for some to believe the lie that God would not allow them to perish. Hoping to escape judgment rather than to take God serious, and accept the truth about their sinful self.

Seriously, how can people accept this when the Bible is clear? There is sound biblical wisdom that may enlighten why people believe what they do. Jesus quotes Isaiah who warned the Israelites that because of their unbelief and non-repentant ways they would be blind to the truth. In addition, they would not be able to recognize it even though it was plainly, shown to them.

> *Therefore I speak to them in parables: because seeing they do not see, and hearing they do not hear, nor do they understand. And in them the prophecy of Isaiah is fulfilled, which says: "Hearing you will hear, and shall not understand; and seeing you will see, and not perceive; for the hearts of this people have grown dull. Their ears are hard of hearing, And their eyes they have closed, Lest they should see with their eyes and hear with their ears, Lest they*

*should understand with their hearts and turn, So that
I should heal them"* (Matthew 13: 13 – 15).

Jesus was comparing the people of His day with those in Isaiah's time. That which occurred in Isaiah's period, also observed in his season. All the miracles that Jesus did were, not enough to cause the people to believe upon Him. They chose to resist the truth of God as illustrated by the closing of their spiritual eyes and ears.

Their hearts had grown dull, just as many have today. The old saying, "Even a blind hog will find an acorn now and then" does not relate here. One must be willing and allow God to remove their blinders, and apply healing balm to their spiritual blindness. Does anyone come to mind?

Beware of False Teachings

Perhaps this accounts for divisions in many churches today and explains why some churches are permissive when it comes to morality. Some churches no longer distinguish a sinner from a believer. They no longer teach Jesus as the only way but rather a way indicating there are numerous ways to heaven.

They use the "homogeneous approach" blending both sinners and saints together using phrases such as, we are all sinners, or we all sin every day, establishing no separation with those redeemed. Churches that fit this category do a disservice to all whom believed saved, putting future seekers of spiritual guidance in danger of judgment.

Buyers beware of those who would offer you the easy way out that requires nothing on your part. Could it be that many church leaders are in the pastorate today as a vocation, and do not qualify as the spiritual leader chosen by God? Are they serving by "election" (God selected them) or by "self will" (they chose themselves). This may account for their apathy concerning their beliefs about morality.

Jesus warns His disciples about false teachers. Our Lord describes those in His generation as serving God only to pull the wool over someone's eyes. They loved to be highly thought of by men enjoying recognition as men of God. Jesus charged them with blocking the truth from others, thus keeping them from entering in.

> *But all their works they do to be seen by men. They make their phylacteries broad and enlarge the borders of their garments. They love the best places at feasts, the best seats in the synagogues, greetings in the marketplaces, and to be called by men, Rabbi, Rabbi. But woe to you, scribes and Pharisees, hypocrites! For you shut up the kingdom of heaven against men; for you neither go in yourselves, nor do you allow those who are entering to go in. Woe to you, scribes and Pharisees, hypocrites! For you devour widows' houses, and for a pretense make long prayers. Therefore you will receive greater condemnation. Woe to you, scribes and Pharisees, hypocrites! For you travel land and sea to win one proselyte, and when he is won, you make him twice as much a son of hell as yourselves* (Matthew 23: 5 - 7, 13 – 15).

In lock step with Christ's condemnation of false teachers, I believe with God's permission confirm in writing this warning. There are no easy ways to say this without being falsely misunderstood. Therefore, I chance my remarks will be, received in the spirit of a loving warning.

There are no "clergyman or church" that can truthfully boast as being more compassionate, loving, forgiving or merciful than God. I repeat there is none, and yet this is happening in churches all across our land today.

For any religious leader either to condone or defend any abominable sin such as, (abortion, homosexual behavior 'either sex', or take part in performing same sex marriages, etc.), are hypocrites.

In reality, they are saying they are more loving and merciful than God is, even though the Creator condemns these sinful acts. I caution those who knowingly follow their example, avoid them at all cost.

As illustrated in the above Scripture they circumvent the word of God pretending to be religious and accept only the parts that pleases them. The rest they ignore or discount as a myth or fable especially the truth pertaining to God's judgments upon such behavior.

Jesus describes them as setting out to *win one proselyte, and when he is* won, *you make him twice as much a son of hell.* It is dangerous to play god no matter who you are. There is the price of repentance to be paid. The non-repentant will go to hell in the end.

Seek the Old Paths

The path must start by accepting the fact that one is lost in sin and needs deliverance. In the Old Testament God speaks against sin, not the sinner, as being an "abomination" to Him. The word abomination carries with it the strong annotation of hating the act of sin while loving the sinner.

For that reason God cannot bear sin neither will He tolerate its stench because it is impervious to all moral and religious decency. To escape punishment a nation or an individual must return to God.

These two words, "Faith and Grace," are important to us, to appreciate the results this has upon us. They are a spiritual marriage that enables the repentant to believe in Jesus Christ. The biblical concept of grace is that of a gift freely given to someone who as a sinner cannot afford nor deserves.

God's grace makes it possible or enables the repentant to believe witnessed by God's mercy. Without mercy, grace would be impossible. Without faith, belief would be impossible as seen in the book of Hebrews. Faith is the realization or confidence in someone even though we cannot see the promise, and yet believe it is real.

The plan of salvation is not a mystery that cannot be understood, but rather simple, so that everyone has an equal opportunity. Therefore, regardless of race, education, or wealth, it is obtainable to those who seek it. Despite man's meddling, whatever the reason, a person cannot seek a lesser way into the kingdom of God and be successful.

God took the first initiative in providing our salvation through Christ Jesus. Now we must take the second step and accept Christ as our savior. There is no other way! Have you taken that first move toward forgiveness? God is not willing that any would perish; caution, He will not violate man's right to choose.

Set Free From Sin

The term *born again* is crucial in understanding our salvation. The words themselves indicate that something must occur. It suggests that a transformation take place within the person similar to their beginning.

At the risk of being redundant, in the book of John we have the story of Nicodemus a Pharisee, a member of the Sanhedrin who came to Jesus by night in pretense to inquire about the miracles that Jesus had been doing. In actuality, he wanted to know if Jesus was the prophesied Messiah, and what he must do to, be saved.

Jesus confirmed His identity, knowing Nicodemus's real intention informs him that he must be born again. *Jesus answered and said to him, "most assuredly, I say to you, unless one is born again, he cannot see the kingdom of God"* (John 3: 3).

Like Nicodemus many today's salvation rest in charitable works, or simply trying to be good. Sadly, missing the importance of what Jesus was saying. He was not referring to man's physical rebirth as the ruler first thought.

Jesus was talking about a spiritual birth a separate birth to man's physical birth. The first birth brought us into this present world; our second birth or new birth makes it possible to live in the world to come.

Using the same general concept, our earthly mother bore pain in our natural birth Jesus suffered our pain for our spiritual birth. One naturally cannot compare equally with the other. Therefore, man has no bragging rights in his redemption, all glory and honor belongs to Christ.

Choices, Choices

From the cradle to the grave, our lives consist of choices defined by the options presented in life. Our entire life made up of choices: what car I drive, where I live, the person I will marry, the career I choose, the friends I have, the clothes I wear, and the list goes on. Some choices are automatic while others come about over a longer period.

We make the right decision and have a measure of happiness in life, or we make wrong choice and live a somewhat less happy life. The most important decision you will ever make is to accept Jesus Christ as your savior. The choosing is yours and yours alone to make. No one can make that for you, not even your parents.

God's plan of salvation is not for just a select few but is available to everyone who sincerely seeks His forgiveness. Sometimes without intending wrong ministers have made it seem more difficult than it really is. *For God so loved the world that He gave His only begotten Son, that whoever believes in Him should not perish but have everlasting life* (John 3: 16).

The steps leading to salvation are simple. Honesty before God and sincerity on our part are the two qualities before progress ever begins. This truth is, expressed, in the Apostle Paul's second letter to the Corinthian Church. *For godly sorrow produces repentance leading to salvation, not to be regretted; but the sorrow of the world produces death* (2 Corinthians 7: 10).

Before, God can bless someone they must humble themselves before Him. The person coming to Christ cannot be proud of their sinful past, but must have a contrite spirit showing evidence of remorse. They must come as a helpless child who is unable to provide for their needs and therefore must rely upon another. His warning is not to take this matter of being born again lightly as many in His day were doing and continues in our day as well.

The Truth Will Set You Free

The greatest bondage of man is not debt, prison, poverty, or illness, but sin; one must begin with the truth about their own sinful condition. *For all have sinned, and fall short of the glory of God. For the wages of sin is death; but the gift of God is eternal life in Christ Jesus our Lord* (Romans 3: 23, 6: 23). The greatest of all liberty that man can experience is freedom from sin.

In the book of John, Jesus is defending himself using the Pharisees' law to establish the truth. The Pharisees believed that no one was free of sin except those who exercised themselves in the law. Jesus refutes this and goes on to reiterate the importance of truth as it pertains to one's true freedom from sin. The truth, He was speaking was about Himself. *And you shall know the truth, and the truth shall make you free. Therefore if the Son makes you free, you shall be free indeed* (John 8: 32, 36),

When trying to understand the steps leading to salvation, remember these are parts of the whole plan at work in our lives, and not necessarily in the order that God uses them to bring about our redemption.

A person must believe that salvation, has been provided for them in Christ, and they cannot save themselves. They must accept as truth, they are a sinner, as the Bible so clearly states; and are doomed unless they accept eternal life through Christ Jesus, by acknowledging they cannot save themselves.

God has made it possible for everyone to spend eternity with Him. There is nothing in, this, life we can do to earn it. Beyond our self, it is always a matter of faith in someone else making it almost impossible to comprehend.

If you have never made that step of faith, or perhaps you have allowed yourself to drift away from the Lord; I ask that you do not put off your salvation one more day. If you are not sure, seek the help of a clergyman or close Christian friend who can explain God's plan of salvation to you making your election sure. God's plan is as simple as this.

> *If you confess with your mouth the Lord Jesus and believe in your heart that God has raised Him from the dead, you will be saved. For with the heart one believes unto righteousness, and with the mouth confession is made unto salvation. For, whoever calls on the name of the Lord shall be saved* (Romans 10: 9 - 10, 13).

The principle foundation here is simple involving confession and belief. The expression *believes unto righteousness* implies that one must turn away from sin and embrace righteousness. A conversion must occur! One must confess with their mouth unto salvation (public affirmation), and believe in their heart (personal acknowledgment) in the Lord Jesus Christ. Their life now reflects Christ likeness rather than a life of sin.

Life is Like a Vapor

Sinners in the hands of an angry God by Jonathan Edwards, one of the most famous sermons ever preached. The sermon initially expounded on July 8, 1741 in Enfield, Connecticut. Had you lived in that day sermons like that would have been the norm rather than the exception.

Here the pastor combined Scripture with imagery to warn his listeners about the reality of, hell, and what it would be like to go there. He stressed that only God's grace keeps us from a devil's hell, and we sinners could be thrown into hell any given moment.

No doubt, his most famous illustration of a sinner in the hands of an angry God liken unto that of a spider held over the pit of hell deserving of its torments. If not for God, the flames would burn the thin thread supporting the sinner hanging there in the balance from plunging to their eternal punishment.

The sermon wherever preached made quiet an impact upon all who heard, and many souls came to Christ to escape eternal punishment.

A truth that none likes to think about, the death rate is one hundred percent; death is not an easy subject to talk about when we live in a society that concentrates primarily on living.

Given the finality of physical death, and the consequences resulting from wrong choices, I hope that everyone will seek the higher road to living, both here, and for the life hereafter.

We only have this one short lifetime, do not miss your opportunity. Eternity is a long time never ending so we need to get it right. *Whereas you do not know what will happen tomorrow. For what is your life? It is even a vapor that appears for a little time and then vanishes away* (James 4: 14).

God has not promised any of us another sunrise although many put off their salvation waiting for a more opportune time. The fact they are born terminal and are judgment bound seems to make little difference.

As a reminder all one has to do is, pass a cemetery, listen to the news, and see that death is man's number one enemy no matter how hard we try to cheat the grim reaper.

One day all will stand before Jesus and give a full account of their life while living here upon earth. Have we reached a point where we no longer fear God, fear death, or fear hell? Only you can answer. Remember, *And as it is appointed for men to die once, but after this the judgment* (Hebrews 9: 27).

Window of Opportunity

The Bible teaches there is a window of opportunity that is open to everyone to whom God calls. Just as God took the initiative and called to Adam and Eve in the Garden-of-Eden, Jesus is standing and knocking upon your hearts door asking to come in.

"Behold, I stand at the door and knock. If anyone hears My voice and opens the door, I will come in to him and dine with him, and he with Me" (Revelations 3: 20). Open the door it is your only way to heaven

After you find Christ, I strongly encourage you find an evangelical church to unite with; and become a part of their family unless you are already attending one Only the truth can keep you free!

DEFINITIONS
The Holy Trinity

The Father - In the Hebrew, these two words adequately describe God. *"Elohim,"* declares God as Creator and absolute ruler of the Universe, emphasizing His impartial justice and moral righteousness. "Adonay," describes His mercy, His Love, and revelation of Himself to humankind seen in the thirteen characteristic qualities of His nature Exodus 34: 6 – 7. The three most quoted attributes describing God's Divine nature are: Omnipresence God is everywhere without bounds or limits; Omniscience God is all knowing past, present and future; and Omnipotent God is all powerful without equal.

The Son - Jesus gives a human face to "Savior" and Christ brings to life the "Anointed One." He is, described, in the book of John as *The Word of God that became flesh and dwelt among us.* He is the only begotten Son of God portraying His deity. He is, called the Son of Man indicating His humanity. He is, called the "Lamb of God" expressing His mission upon earth to give His life that we might receive forgiveness from our sins.

The Holy Spirit - The Holy Spirit is both a power and an influence in the world today. He is the one who will convict the world of sin, and of righteousness and of judgment and purges the heart from all sin. The Holy Spirit bears fruit in those in Christ, *But the fruit of the Spirit is love, joy, peace, longsuffering, kindness, goodness, faithfulness, gentleness, self-control. Against such there is no law* (Galatians 5: 22 – 23).

Holiness Terms

Christian Perfection - Means completeness of our Christian character and our possession of spiritual graces that makes it possible to live a victorious life in Christ.

Entire Sanctification – Means to cleanse from all sin including the carnal nature.

Full Salvation – Means that Christ is fully adequate and has provided for all-of-our sin problem.
Second Blessing – Is the term used by John Wesley to point out that entire sanctification is a second work of grace.

Other Terms

Attributes – Are those qualities belonging to God that humans can never possess. The most common describing who God is, are; Omnipresence - Always present everywhere all the time; Omnipotent - Unlimited power throughout the universe without equal; Omniscience – Perfect knowledge past, present, and future, without equal.
Born Again - Is a term that Jesus used when talking to Nicodemus describing the process of the spiritual birth that must take place among all who accept Christ as their Lord.
Bondsman – Is a person who of their own free will becomes a slave to their master.
Carnal Nature – Is the sin nature that all humanity is born with that needs changing. The carnal nature produces such sinful behaviors as evil thoughts, adulteries, fornications, murders, thefts, covetousness, wickedness, deceit, lewdness, an evil eye, blasphemy, pride, and foolishness and more.
Confession – Is to pour out ones soul to another holding nothing back, as to clear one's conscience. Jesus Christ is the gateway to receive our confession.
Consecration – Is the perfect submission of the soul to God.
Eradication - Is the elimination of the carnal nature in the life of the believer upon complete surrender to the will of God. This witnessed in the life of the follower of Christ when the conflict between the flesh and the spirit ends. This will not end temptations or trials in one's Christian walk as some believe.
Forgiveness – To wipe the slate clean, and never to hold against again, is to completely forget and erase all wrongdoing.

Grace - Is the unmerited favor of God that allows the sinner to believe in God relating to his redemption, which he cannot earn by works or deeds. Grace ensures in man what the law was unable to do.

Heaven – Is, revealed, as a real place by Jesus, John 14: 2 – 3 and was, seen by the Apostle John in a vision Revelations 21; 2. John describes heaven as the New Jerusalem prepared as a bride adorned for her husband. This describes heaven as a place of beauty, peace, joy, happiness, and our eternal abode with the Lord Jesus Christ. No wickedness or evil will be, allowed.

Hell – Is the eternal abode, of all who died in rebellious sin against, God. It is a literal place described as unquenchable fire, the lake of fire, outer darkness, and the wrath of God. It is a place of torment as witnessed by a certain rich man Luke 16: 19 – 31. All those who are condemned to this place are never to come out.

Holiness - Is a term used to describe one who separates or withdraws from worldly pleasures and pledges to live a life of purity and righteousness before God.

Humble – Is showing respect for others, both in attitude, and behavior.

Law - The law for all practical purposes is, embodied in the Ten Commandments. The law summarized, God's, will for man in worship of, Him, and how to live in harmony with each, other. The law becomes his school, master, and shows man his sinfulness before God.

Man – He was, created, a little lower than the angles, and is earth-born meaning he was, formed from the dust of the earth and became a living soul. For this reason makes him a citizen of two worlds,' heaven and earth Psalm 8: 5 and Exodus 2: 7.

Man is, endowed, with free will in his ability to choose between right or wrong, good or evil. Because of his sin nature, he must be, redeemed through Christ Jesus. In view of that, he must give an account of himself to God determining where he will spend eternity.

Pride – Is the opposite of humility, displaying a sense of arrogance, or self-importance., Pride can cause a person to become haughty and become unyielding. In biblical language, pride was, seen, as the forerunner of personal, destruction.

Righteousness – Simply stated is right living before God reflecting honesty, decency, virtue, and modesty, living by a moral code conceived according to the Word of God to be correct and just.

Salvation - This embodies the process of saving, or rescuing someone beyond their means or ability. It is through God's unmerited grace that makes one's redemption possible. Salvation is through grace initiated by faith and not by our works that any can boast. It simply means to salvage that which has been, damaged and restore it to its rightful place.

Sanctification – While holiness refers to the state or condition of Godlikeness, sanctification describes the act or process by which they are to partake of this quality. The work of sanctification includes both the human act of consecration and the Divine act of cleansing.

The central idea of Christianity is the purification of the heart from sin and its renewal in the moral image of God. This begins in regeneration (being saved), and is called initial sanctification and is completed in entire sanctification or being filled with the Holy Spirit.

Satan – Is, described, in Genesis as the serpent. In the Hebrew, Satan means "the accuser." The prophet Isaiah describes Lucifer as a fallen angel. He is the chief of liars and tempter of the human race to lead them away from God. The devil is the prince of this world as ruler of darkness and lawlessness. He ultimately will be, cast, into hell and all who follow him.

Saved – Refers to what takes place regarding one's salvation. Someone is lost and now found.

Separate – Means to come apart, to be different from the world.

Sin - Is the willful transgression to the known will of God as committed by Adam and Eve in the garden when they took of the forbidden fruit Genesis 2: 16 - 17, 3: 1 – 6. Because of their sin, all humanity is born with a carnal nature that separates him from God. This sin nature places man in a category by himself leaving, God, no choice but to banish him to an eternity in hell, unless he repents and accepts God's conditions of salvation.

Sinner - Is singular defining the one who commits acts of sins. Sinners in the plural accurately define the state of all humankind regardless of race without exception prior to their redemption.

Suppression – Means to suppress the carnal spirit in lieu of having it removed. This is what many attempt to do without fully consecrating their life to God. You cannot suppress the carnal nature for very long and at the most unlikely time will show itself.

Transgression - Is an act committed against a law or command or moral code. The person committing such an act is, called, the transgressor.

Misconceptions of Christian Perfection

Holiness – Is not absolute perfection; only God is absolute.

Holiness – Is not Adams perfection before his fall. Man is under the curse of physical death.

Holiness - Is not perfect health or instant wealth as some might choose to believe.

Holiness – Is not angelic perfection; we are a little lower than the angels are.

Holiness – Is not perfect knowledge past, present or future; only God is omniscience.

Holiness – Is not the use of unlimited power; only God is omnipotent.

Holiness – Is not human infallibility; only God is infinite, man is finite.

Holiness – Is not the absence of frustration, mistakes, heartache, suffering, temptations, or trials.

Holiness – Is not suppression of such as; anger, jealously, envy, covetousness or pride.

Holiness – Is not a one-time filling of the Holy Spirit.

LESSON OUTLINE
INTRODUCTION

The lesson outlines objective is to provide a miniature review of each chapter to aid the student as a refresher or take part in a study group. There are questions at the end of each chapter to aid in the discovery of truth/deeper learning experience. .

Holiness without a doubt is the righteous focal point found in both the Old and New Testament. It was God's intent in the beginning with Adam and it is God's will today. Many churches today make plain its reality and enjoy the blessing of holiness while others fail to embrace its truth. Jesus referring to the Holy Spirit said, *"And when He has come, He will convict the world of sin, and of righteousness, and of judgment"* (John 16: 8).

My heartfelt request for you is whether you are in a study group or alone that you will be open to the Holy Spirit and the truth revealed in His Word.

CHAPTER 1
Opinions Matter

Before you begin this study or any other book, do not be eager to believe every teacher or preacher just because of their, claim to be sent by God. Check everything against God's Word to ensure its truth. *All Scripture is given by inspiration of God, and is profitable for doctrine, for reproof, for correction, for instruction in righteousness* (2 Timothy 3: 16).

Try the spirits:
> *Beloved, do not believe every spirit, but test the spirits, whether they are of God; because many false prophets have gone out into the world* (1 John 4: 1).

Invite the Holy Spirit to enlighten your mind to the truth as you study His Word. Be open to the truth as taught in Scripture.

Age-old debate

Many differences debated in churches today are unprovable based upon assumption rather than God's Word. There will always be differences among churches regarding living a Spirit filled life. Ones beliefs often measured by his or her spiritual maturity influences ones thinking. The age-old question; am I saved or am I lost depends upon your point of view based upon perception of Scriptures.

Example, John Calvin taught unconditional election; Jacob Arminius taught that falling from grace was possible because our election was conditional based upon personal faith. To date this continues among Christians, neither side willing to budge from their position. A careful look at God's Word provides the answer and leaves the follower of Christ with a clear witness concerning his spiritual standing before God.

There is only one judge

The Holy Spirit is the only one who is capable of doing this in the life of the believer. His job is to convict the world of sin, of righteousness, and of judgment. It is wise to follow the prompting of the Holy Spirit.

We are one body sharing responsibility

The challenges Christian's encounters today in a society gone mad are difficult to say the least. The body of Christ should encourage each other in the Lord as instructed and never take the spiritual wellbeing of a fellow believer lightly we need each other. *But exhort one another daily, while it is called 'today,' lest any of you be hardened through the deceitfulness of sin* (Hebrews 3: 13).

Review questions
Why do opinions matter?
How can we know if it is true?
What are some of the debates among churches today?
What other helps are available to know the truth?
How can we help a fellow Christian in their walk width Christ?

CHAPTER 2
God in all Creation

The First verse in the Bible is without doubt one of the most prolific verses found in Scripture. The first three chapters are probably the most important chapters in the Bible. Before doubting creation, it would humble those who think themselves wise to read Job chapters thirty-eight through forty-one where God asked Job a series of questions that only a person who was present at that moment of creation could answer.

**In the beginning*:*

In the beginning God created the heavens and the earth (Genesis 1: 1).

Evolution

The word Evolution comes from the Latin "*Evolvere"* indicating to change gradually. Many today accept Darwin' teaching of evolution over creation causing many to doubt God as Creator. Doubts can lead someone eventually to deny God, as did Darwin.

Evolutionary influence

Influence has no boundary. Darwin's theory of natural evolution denies the existence of a Creator God, and no longer taught in our schools as a theory, although unprovable, but as scientific fact.

Creation

The Hebrew word for "Book of Creation" is *Sefer Maaseh Bereshith.* We recognize it best by its Greek name *Genesis* meaning origin. The book is unique in the fact that it declares God as the creator apart from all things that exists, and gives details to the origin of man, and his relationship to God, tying all humankind together from Adam.

Elohim

The traditional Jewish teaching of the Hebraic word used to describe God in His creative and judgment role in the universe. This puts God in a category all by Himself without equal. There is no higher power.

Adonay

The Hebrew word used to reveal God in His association with humankind. He is seen as Lord, Master or Owner. He is also, seen for His love and mercy, and impartial judgment.

Review questions

Do you agree with verse one, and why?

What are some reasons people doubt God?

Can you list other things that influence people today?

Does the biblical view of creation make sense and why?

Do these two thoughts confirm who God is and are they still relevant today?

CHAPTER 3
Beginning of Life

This describes man in his actual physical process enabling him to be a rational being capable of love and having communion with God. This spiritual union with God was to be a holy communion without sin.

The breath of life:

> *And the Lord God formed man of the dust of the ground, and breathed into his nostrils the breath of life; and man became a living being* (Genesis 2: 7).

The first family

> *Therefore a man shall leave his father and mother and be joined to his wife, and they shall become one flesh* (Genesis 2: 24).

The union between a man and a woman now becomes one flesh and grows to become closer than their biological family. This is an important concept associated to holiness establishing one's fidelity to each other.

In addition, the wife has no greater honor than to love and respect her husband, the husband has no greater duty than to love and protect his wife above his own life. Just as a husband and wife are to be completely devoted to each other, we are to be faithful to God in the same manner.

Man created an intellectual being

In the Hebrew, the word formed *"vayyitzer"* is written with two "yods;" therefore, man was created with a "Yetzer Tob and a Yetzer Ra" interpreted means capable of doing both good and evil being accountable, having to do with choices they make.

Freedom of choice

Freedom of choice is a wonderful gift and carries with it certain responsibility exacting consequences. When we disobey the known will of God, as did Adam and Eve we cause conflict to surface brought about by our disobedience.

> *And the Lord God commanded the man, saying, "of every tree of the garden you may freely eat; but of the tree of the knowledge of good and evil you shall not eat, for in the day that you eat of it you shall surely die"* (Genesis 2: 16 – 17).

Source of temptation

When we are enticed, do not say that we are, tempted by God. Each are, tempted when, they, are drawn away by his or her, own desires and enticed. Wrongful temptations come from only one primal source. Temptations come in all sizes and shapes to gain our attraction. They are not limited to age, education, social status or race. James the brother of our Lord makes this clear James 1: 13, 17.

Web of deceit

Deception by any means is still deception no matter how you sugar coat it. Satan is a master at this and we are no match for him on our own as Eve was about to find out.

> *Now the serpent was more cunning than any beast of the field which the Lord God had made. And he said to the woman, "has God indeed said, you shall not eat of every tree of the garden?"' And the woman said to the serpent, "we may eat the fruit of the trees of the garden; but of the fruit of the tree which is in the midst of the garden, God has said, you shall not eat it, nor shall you touch it, least you die". Then the serpent said to the woman, "you will not surely*

die. For God knows that in the day you eat of it your eyes will be opened, and you will be like God, knowing good and evil." So when the woman saw that the tree was good for food, that it was pleasant to the eyes, and a tree desirable to make one wise, she took of its fruit and ate. She also gave to her husband with her, and he ate (Genesis 3: 1 – 6).

Be sure your sins will find you out

The Psalmist David declared there is no place man can hide from God, and that God has perfect knowledge of man and all his activities both good and bad. Nothing can be hid that will remain covered our sins will find us out eventually. The Bible is clear on this, *But if you do not do so, then take note, you have sinned against the LORD; and be sure your sin will find you out* (Numbers 32: 23).

Review questions

What are some of the world's view of the creation of man and do you agree?
Do you agree with this if not why not?
List both good and evil humankind is capable of doing.
Are we responsible for the choices we make?
How can we be tempted, and how can we avoid its snare?

CHAPTER 4
Consequences of Sin

Actions always lead to consequences and can be either good or bad depending upon the choices we make in life. Paul wrote to the Romans, because of Adams sin "Many were made sinners." He did not leave us without hope because he also wrote about Christ's obedience, *by one man's disobedience many were made sinners, so also by one Man's obedience many will be made righteous* (Romans 5: 19)

Man's rebellious nature:

For to be carnally minded is death, but to be spiritually minded is life and peace. Because the carnal mind is enmity against God; for it is not subject to the law of God, nor indeed can be (Romans 8: 6 – 7).

Results of disobedience

The first command given to man was not to eat "of the tree of knowledge" followed by the consequences "you shall surely die" expressing the promise of death. Two deaths occurred, man's natural death and spiritual death. While God will not violate man's right to choose right or wrong, man has an obligation that demands his obedience to the will of God.

A new nature given

Because of Adam's sin his sinless nature was altered he now possessed a carnal or fleshly nature. As a result, Eve also possessed a carnal or fleshly nature since they chose to disobey God of their own free will. For this reason, they were no longer subject to the law of God that one must obey Him *Because the carnal mind is enmity against God* (Romans 8: 7a).

Separated from God

Sin causes man to leave God's presence when we consider that God drove Adam and Eve from the garden. Only repentance can restore this broken relationship.

Physical death occurred

Because of his disobedience, he now became a mortal being and the sentence of death placed upon him and all that follows.

The first act of murder

The first act of murder occurred for the reason of man's sin nature, when Cain killed Able. His carnal nature acted out in a rage of jealousy against his brother.

All have sinned

No one can boast they, have never sinned. *For all have sinned and fall short of the glory of God* (Romans 3: 23).

The great commission

Jesus in His great commission made it the church's responsibility to enlighten the sinner about the truth of God and His mercy. The danger facing churches today is compromise. It would appear that the church has lost its first love of making disciples and are substituting a feel good gospel in its place. New ideologies replacing the gospel of salvation are taking center stage as the new focus of worship.

Review questions
What are some of the consequences of sin?
Is God just to punish?
Is "being good" enough to get into heaven, why not?
What are some of the dangers facing the 21st century church?

CHAPTER 5
Law and Grace

There never were one standard yesterday in the Old Testament under "the Law" and a new standard today in the New Testament under "Grace." The laws of the Old Testament and grace in the New Testament complement each other. Jesus confirms the law is still valid therefore will not be, abolished. Paul taught that without the law, we would certainly never know that we are sinners.

Can you imagine living in a society where every man became a law unto himself? What could you expect from a society living under those conditions? Laws serve a meaningful purpose allowing humankind to live together for the common good of each person.

God's laws are true:
> *Blessed is the man who walks not in the counsel of the ungodly, Nor stands in the path of sinners, Nor sits in the seat of the scornful; But his delight is in the law of the Lord, And in His law he meditates day and night* (Psalm 1: 1 – 2).

The law is the unwavering guide to what constitutes good and evil. It is not man's instincts, his reason or socially accepted practices, as many rely upon today. In his hour of temptation, often calls light darkness and darkness light. God's law has always been a point of contention between some Christians who believe the Old Testament law is not contemporary today.

Without partiality

God is without partiality, only humankind shows partiality. *Jesus Christ is the same yesterday, today, and forever* (Hebrews 13: 8).

Old Testament Law

To help comprehend Old Testament law as it pertained to the Jewish people I have divided them into three parts to reinforce our understanding of their value (Commandments, Statutes, and Customs and traditions).

Commandments

Commandments include any demand, given by God, reflecting His righteousness. There usually preceded with "Thou shall, or shall not," followed by the command instructions. These are an obligation and not an option to disobey.

All commandments need grounding in Scripture. The most familiar example of these is the laws reflected in the Ten Commandments governed by God's sovereign righteous moral principles. Are commandments still valid today or they outdated?

Statutes

Statutes are decrees ordained by God that we are to observe though human reason cannot define why. Example; why were the children of Israel, forbidden to eat meat of certain animals?

Customs and traditions

Religious, customs and traditions handed down one generation to the next typically defines the teachings of the church illustrated in their worship practices.

God's grace is essential

Without God's grace, we would not be able to accept the gift of salvation. Man does not possess the power or means to save his self and therefore must rely upon the grace of God to provide this. *For by grace you have been saved through faith, and that not of yourselves; it is the gift of God* (Ephesians 2: 8).

Prevenient grace

Is generally expressed "going before or preceding" someone providing man with freedom which to make choices that he might not otherwise have or make.

Saving or redeeming grace

It is the endless co-operation between the human will and God's grace until repentance takes on faith, which makes possible our salvation.

Continual or sustaining grace

It is through God's providence in our Christian walk we are, sustained. This otherwise, cannot be achieved in our own strength. When we confess our weakness then we become strong to endure until the end. Although God never forces man to exercise his faith, the power to act is his choice.

Understanding the law through grace by faith

The law of works does not oppose grace by faith. There is a correlation between both that works in harmony. Holiness goes beyond keeping rules governing our conduct. Works and faith supports each other in keeping holiness alive so our spiritual lives will not become vain and imaginary.

Keeping our conscience clear

Some churches may choose works opposed to grace while others stress grace without works. Often our conscience terrified by the sense of doing wrong by simply keeping the law of works, by ignoring grace, or by ignoring the law at the expense of grace. There should be a balance between the two truths. To the careful reader the book of James is better, caught, than taught. James blends the two together showing that one is impossible without the other.

Review questions

Does God have different standards for moral living?
What are the benefits and what are the dangers of these?
(Commandments, Statues, Customs/traditions)
What have you learned about grace?
What have you learned about the law through grace?

CHAPTER 6
Holiness God's Command

Many often overlook this verse, despite the fact that it implies we are to strive for a peaceful coexistence with those around us. We are to live holy in a continual life of heart purity separated from the worldly pleasures that God condemns in His Word. *Pursue peace with all people, and holiness, without which no one will see the Lord* (Hebrews 12: 14).

Holiness is attainable:
> *For I am the Lord your God. You shall therefore consecrate yourselves, and you shall be holy; for I am holy* (Leviticus 11: 44a).

Yesterday and today

To substantiate the same requirement of behavior involving holiness between the Old and New Testament binding both periods together found in Leviticus and I Thessalonians. Both Scriptures are comparable in meaning; both texts are equally identical in purpose. It is unthinkable to believe that God has a double standard for His people or would require something without providing the means to obtain.

Royal command

The words *Hear, O Israel: The Lord our God, the Lord is one* (Deuteronomy 6: 4) has been said to enshrine Judaism's greatest contribution to the religious thought of all generations. Without an understanding and appreciation for the Jewish teaching and their deep respect and worship of their creator enriches our worship.

Longevity of holiness

The recital of the Shema was a vital part of the Jews regular daily worship in the temple. The Shema became the first prayer of early childhood and the last prayer of the dying. This is referred, to as Israel's "Watchword and confession of Faith." One should have a clear understanding and not a confused or confounded knowledge of the duties and teachings of their faith.

Imitation of God

The Jews believe that man was not only to worship God, but was to imitate Him in their walk of, life. Their lives were to be a carbon copy of their Creator reflected in both Old and New Testaments.

A kingdom of priests

According to Rabbinical teaching this denotes a kingdom whose citizens are all priests living wholly in God's service. This was

Israel's highest mission. God calls all of us to be His witness to the world.

Role models needed

We are living in a day when this generation more than ever needs heroes or role models to look up to. When you think of a hero or role model who comes to mind? A hero is someone who is, admired, for his or her bravery, and character, or achievements. A role model is different and someone that is a good example worthy of our imitation. The greatest role model is Jesus Christ whom we ought to imitate.

Review questions

How important is holiness to you?
What part does holiness play in this kingdom?
What is your definition of a role model?

CHAPTER 7
God's Blueprint

God has not left us without instructions, support, or guidance as the verse in Isaiah points out. All we have to do is pay attention to His still small voice. As with any blueprint, the master architect has a design in mind reflected in his drawings viewed as a guided process.

This is the way:

> *Your ears shall hear a word behind you, saying, "This is the way, walk in it, Whenever you turn to the right hand Or whether you turn to the left"* (Isaiah 30: 21).

God the master Creator has a plan for our life, revealed in His Word. That is to live a holy life and enjoy unlimited fellowship with Him. Anything less than this is undesirable. Christian Perfection is not to be confused with or to imply that one never makes an unintentional mistake.

Consecration

Is our willingness to submit our self without reservation to the service of God? All that results from our consecration as an act of God, results in our willingness to submit to the Lordship of Jesus

Christ. Our willingness to submit our self unconditionally without reservation to the service of God implies a question mark (?) defined by this unselfish act of consecration upon the consecrated.

Separation

The expression in the term separate implies to come apart, to be different from the world. We cannot serve two masters *God and mammon* (Matthew 6: 24) as our Lord taught. The Apostle Paul describes one's separation depicting the state or condition of Godlikeness 2 Corinthians 6: 14 – 17.

Sanctification

The Israelites believe the basis for sanctification is, found, in the term *You shall be holy; for I am holy* (Leviticus 11: 44). This explains one's obligation to sanctify or separate one's self or come apart as a prerequisite for their capacity to receive the Holy Spirit in His fullness I Thessalonians 5: 22 – 24.

Law vs. grace

For what the law could not do in that it was weak through the flesh, God did by sending His own Son (Romans 8: 3a).

We need to understand the arguments between the weakness of the "Law" of the Old Testament; and strength of "Grace" in the New Testament, and how each applies.

Judgment without prejudice

Paul in his letter to the Romans acknowledged that we must all stand before the judgment seat of Christ. God will judge without prejudice according to the deeds that we have done here upon earth.

Review questions

What is the difference between a sin and a mistake?

What does consecration and separation have to do with sanctification?

(Consecration/separation, Sanctification)

Would you judge humankind differently, why?

CHAPTER 8
Highway to Heaven

Isaiah the prophet when forth telling the coming of Jesus and His redemptive purpose compares it to a highway. The road leading to heaven is a single highway, and is Holy, and all who walk on it shall be holy. There is only one road, that will get you to heaven, and that road is Jesus Christ. There will be no excuse accepted for not getting onboard this highway-to-heaven.

Highway of holiness:

> *A highway shall be there, and a road, and it shall be called the Highway of Holiness., The unclean shall not pass over it, But it shall be for others. Whoever walks the road, although a fool, Shall not go astray. No lion shall be there, Nor shall any ravenous beast go up on it; It shall not be found there. But the redeemed shall walk there* (Isaiah 35: 8 – 9).

Conformation

Anything as important to humankind as salvation, especially with where we will spend eternity would like conformation along the way that we are the children of God. Paul led by the Holy Spirit wrote to the church giving them comfort. *The Spirit Himself bears witness with our spirit that we are children of God* (Romans 8: 16).

All-encompassing promise of power

Jesus prior to ascending back to heaven promised His disciples a comforter and as a sign, *He breathed on them, and said to them, "Receive the Holy Spirit"* (John 20: 22).

Incompatible companions

Paul describes a war that goes on between the spirit and flesh in that what one would like to do they cannot. The things they should not do they find themselves doing. *Walk in the Spirit, and you shall not fulfill the lust of the flesh. For the flesh lusts against the Spirit, and the Spirit against the flesh* (Galatians 5: 16 -17a).

Review question

How would you explain salvation to someone?

What does the highway mean to you in spiritual terms?

CHAPTER 9
Our Journey Begins

The Psalmist David in the twenty-third Psalm recognized that God is a provider, travel companion, and guardian to those who puts their trust in Him.

Walk before me:

> *When Abram was ninety-nine years old, the Lord appeared to Abram and said to him, "I am Almighty God; walk before Me and be blameless"*
> {'be blameless' is sometimes translated as 'be thou wholehearted'} (Genesis 17: 1).

With Abraham, who was ninety-nine when God spoke those words to him could only imply one thing. He was commanding Abram to walk before Him to show determination, to be open with nothing to hide. This single-minded expression was a unique expression of obedient, endurance, and determination to be holy before God.

As in any adventure, there must be a starting point and a destination that concludes one's journey. I like to think that my Christian experience is both, a journey and an adventure. The voyage because have not reached destination; and the adventure, lies in the mystery as life unfolds. I like to think that my combined secular vocation and Christian experience can be both a voyage and an adventure.

A new birth

A friend once told me that he did not understand what born again meant. He is not alone. The new birth is crucial in understanding our redemption as Jesus told Nicodemus because his salvation rested in the law. The term *born again* is crucial in understanding the meaning of salvation.

The first step toward God

In order to be, saved, a person must first acknowledge the truth that he or she is a sinner apart from God. Honesty before God and sincerity on our part are the two qualities, which is necessary before the redemptive process can ever begin. The steps leading to salvation are not complicated, as some have tried to make it today.

Time to prepare our heart

After we are, saved, by grace, there is a time between being, saved, until we are, sanctified holy. From the moment one is, saved, until sanctified the time table will vary depending upon the individual and their willingness to allow the Holy Spirit access to their life.

Sacrifice required

Paul an intellectual Scholar in the Mosaic Law draws a parallel of Old Testament animal sacrifices ordained by God; replaced in the New Testament with a living human sacrifice. The focus now moves from the animal to the human with the exception that only a living sacrifice is accepted. *I beseech you therefore, brethren, by the mercies of God, that you present your bodies a living sacrifice, holy, acceptable to God, which is your reasonable service* (Romans 12: 1).

No substitute allowed

Many today are offering up a variety of things in substitute for old fashion holy living without giving themselves fully to Christ. One cannot offer to God in worship anything less than his all. Israel tried to do this and found it was displeasing to God. *But cursed be the deceiver who has in his flock a male, and takes a vow, But sacrifices to the Lord what is blemished* (Malachi 1: 14).

Exemplary example

This command was, given, to Abraham when he was Ninety-nine years old. *I am Almighty God; walk before Me and be blameless* (Genesis 17:1b). Incidentally, serves as a good example for us to follow. Abraham's obedience to walk before God was about to receive, his most crucial test known to man, Genesis 22: 1 – 2. In Abraham's case, his willingness to sacrifice Isaac and surrender unto God what is even dearer than his own life.

Review questions

How would you describe your Christian journey?

What does the new birth mean to you?
Can you name some substitutes people use?

CHAPTER 10
Filled With His Spirit

This chapter will address the importance of how it applies in the life of the believer. On the Day of Pentecost, Peter standing with the eleven confirmed what took place was spoken by the prophet Joel. What is interesting Pentecost is interrelated to the Old Testament "Feast of Weeks," traditionally known as festival of Shavuot. Both are, celebrated, fifty days following a special event in history.

Day of Pentecost:
> *When the Day of Pentecost had fully come, they were all with one accord in one place. And they were all filled with the Holy Spirit* (Acts 2: 1, 4a).

The Spirit of truth

In the sixteenth chapter of John Jesus declares the future work of the Holy Spirit in the world and in the life of His followers after He returns to Heaven. In chapter seventeen, He prays for Himself, His disciples, and all future believers. One word that stands out among the rest is "truth." Jesus validates God's Word is true, when He prays,
And for their sakes I sanctify Myself, that they also may be sanctified by the truth (John 17: 19).

Before and after Pentecostal behavior

There is some misunderstanding concerning the disciples not being, saved prior to Pentecost. This theory does not agree with Jesus High Priestly Prayer John 17: 6 – 19. Jesus knowing that He was soon leaving this world asks the Father to keep them, as He had kept them in His Father's name, losing none except the son of perdition that the, Scripture, might be fulfilled. He asks, for them to be, sanctified, by His truth, which occurred on the day of Pentecost.

Sanctification a second work of grace

It is impossible for the sinner to know the depth of his sin problem when he first comes to Christ to be, saved. He does not know that he needs cleansing from his carnal nature until later as witnessed by this example:

> *Now when the apostles who were at Jerusalem heard that Samaria had received the word of God, they sent Peter and John to them, who, when they had come down prayed for them that they might receive the Holy Spirit. For as yet He had fallen upon none of them. They had only been baptized in the name of the Lord Jesus. Then they laid hands on them, and they received the Holy Spirit* (Acts 8: 14 - 17).

The greatest example

The greatest example of selfless devotion is, seen, in the life of Christ in the Garden-of- Gethsemane prior to Him going to the cross.

We will never achieve this measure of devotion, but it should serve as an example of what devotion is all about.

Bondservant forever

The bondservant to Christ, whom several disciples referred themselves, is similar to the meaning found in the Old Testament Exodus 21: 1 - 6. Example, Paul was a bondservant to Jesus meaning forever. In the Old Testament the, bond servant, could be released in the seventh year of his service called the year of Jubilee or he could remain a bondman to his master for life depending upon the circumstance of his choosing.

Victory in Jesus

You want victory, real victory, then, you must do as Jesus taught us, come, and put everything upon the altar of God dying out to self. Only then will you have real victory.

Review questions

What events do we celebrate today that we consider important to our heritage?

Should the church be different from the world, how?

Is sanctification necessary and why?

What does a bondservant mean to you?

CHAPTER 11
Our Final Destination

People are a creature of two worlds. In this world, he is only passing through, and time is limited upon this earth. The second is eternal where there will be no sunset or limit of time. It will be eternal. It is much easier to believe in a loving God who does not punish rather than a just God who would condemn someone to hell. The truth is no one has to go there because in His mercy God provided a way of escape.

Heaven or hell:

> *His Lord said to him, "Well done, good and faithful servant; you have been faithful over a few things, I will make you ruler over many things. Enter into the joy of your Lord. Cast the unprofitable servant into outer darkness. There will be weeping and gnashing of teeth"* (Matthew 25:23, 30).

If you have ever had doubts concerning eternity, here Jesus uses the parable of talents to describe an absolute infinite truth.

Heaven

Heaven is, seen, as a separate location from the earth as a division of the universe. John in Revelation describes it as the "New Jerusalem." It is a literal place where the redeemed will reside throughout eternity with Christ. Words cannot describe its beauty and all that heaven offers to its inhabitants. Of all the beauty heaven offers to those who go there, hell offers just the opposite in proportion.

Hell

Hell is a literal place described as a place of weeping, gnashing of teeth, everlasting punishment, torment, and unquenchable fire to mention a few. Those who inhabit will never leave and their punishment will endure forever.

Who is responsible?

Man alone is responsible for his own actions because he is, given, freedom of choice. Man was, made separate from the animals in that he was, gifted like His Creator possessing moral character, immortality, and freedom of will.

The finality of hell

Jesus describes a great gulf fixed between heaven and hell that will not allow passage from one to the other or the reverse. After the judgment, there is never a mention of Jesus ever visiting hell, or having anything to do with those in hell.

Review questions

Is heaven real, why?
Is hell real, why?
Is heaven and hell eternally final?
How would you warn/tell someone?

SCRIPTURE REFERENCES

Old Testament:

Genesis [1:1] [1:3] [1:4] [1:5, 8, 13] [1:14] [1:26] [1:31] [2:4] [2:7] [2:15-16] [2:17] [2:16-17] [2:18-22] [2:24] [3:1-6] [3:9b] [3:10b] [3:11] [3:15] [3:16] [3:17b] [3:19b] [3:22-24] [14:19, 22] [17:1] [22:1-2 [25:30-34]
Exodus [2:7] [34:6-7]
Leviticus [8:22-23] [11:44] [11:44a, 19:1-2]
Numbers [32:23]
Deuteronomy [6:4-5] [6:6-9]
Joshua [24:15a]
Judges [16:6-21] [21:25b]
1 Samuel [16:7b]
2 Samuel [12:10]
2 Kings [1:10-12]
Job [38:2-11] [40:2] [42:2-3]
Psalm [1:1-2] [8:4a] [8:4] [8:5] [8:5-8] [9:17] [18:32] [23:1, 4a 5a] [33:6a] [51:5] [90:2- 4] [139:1-12] [147:4]
Proverbs [22:8]
Ecclesiastes [1:9b] [11:3] [12:7]
Isaiah [1:2-4, 10-20] [30:21, 35:8b] [35:8-9] [40:6] [40:8]
Joel [2:28-32a]
Zechariah [4:6]
Malachi [1:6-8, 14]

New Testament

Matthew [3:5-6, 11-12] [4:1-11] [5:13-16] [5:17-19] [6:9-13] [6:19-21] [7:1-2] [7:12]
[7:13-14] [10:37a] [12:32-34a] [13:13-15] [16:26] [22:36-40] [22:37] [22:37-39] [22:37-40] [23:5-7, 13-15] [24:35] [25:23, 30] [26:36-39] [28:18-20]
Mark [8:31-33] [10:35-45] [14:36b] [16:15-16]
Luke [9:51-56] [9:62] [10:2] [16:19-31]

John [1:1-3] [1:3] [3:3-4] [3:5-7] [3:16] [3:18, 5:24, 6:40, 47] [6:38] [8:32, 36] [9:31] [12:24-26] [13:36-38] [14:2-3] [14:16, 16:13] [15:5] [16:8] [16:8, 13] [16:13, 17:17-19] [17:6-19] [20:21-22]

Acts [2:-4:] [2:1-4] [2:1-18] [2:17-21] [8:14-17] [9:1-6, 10-17] [10:34] [19:1-6] [26:12-18]

Romans [1:17] [1:29-32] [2:11] [3:23] [3:23, 6:23] [5:19a] [6:1-2, 7:19] [6:12-14] [6:15-23] [7:7] [8:3-4] [8:6] [8:6-7] [8:16] [10:9-10, 13] [12:1] [12:1-2] [13:1-7]

1 Corinthians [2:9] [2:14] [3:1-4] [4:2-4] [6:9-10] [15:31]
2 Corinthians [5:17, 6:17-18, 7:1] [6:14-17] [7:1] [7:10] [12:9a]
Galatians [5:16-17] [5:22] [5:22-23]
Ephesians [2:8] [5:1] [5:22-25] [5:27]
Philippians [2:5-6] [3:9]
1 Thessalonians [4:3-5, 7-8] [5:22] [5:22-24]
2 Thessalonians [2:3, 9-12] [3:6-10] [3:10-11]
2 Timothy [3:5a] [3:16]
Titus [2:7-8]
Hebrews [2:6] [3:13] [3:12-19, 4:1-2] [9:27] [12:14] [13:8]
James [1:13-17] [2:14, 17-18, 26] [4:7] [4:14] [21:26]
1 Peter [1:13-17] [1:16] [1:24-25] [2:5]
2 Peter [2:22b] [3:9]
1 John [3:4-9] [4:1]
Revelation [3:20] [20:11-15] [20:13-15] [21:2] [21:22-27] [22:]

PART II

A NATION IN TURMOIL

9-1-1

CONTENTS

INTRODUCTION — 162

CHAPTER 1 — 168
The Beginning
A Long Journey

CHAPTER 2 — 181
A Nation in Crisis
9 – 1 - 1

CHAPTER 3 — 194
America vs. Canaan
A Country without God

CHAPTER 4 — 207
Abortion
America's Holocaust

CHAPTER 5 — 219
Judgment
God Has the Final Word

SCRIPTURE REFERENCES — 240

INTRODUCTION

A Nation in Turmoil is an acknowledgment to the *bread of tears* taken from the Psalm. In the fifth verse, the writer describes God's apportion of punishment to the children of Israel for their disobedience revealing; *You have fed them with the bread of tears, and given them tears to drink in great measure* (Psalms 80: 5).

In other words, there was no rest, no comfort, only loneliness and hopelessness during their Babylonian captivity. Their beloved city *Jerusalem* lay in ruin, and they could only complain of the cruelty they were suffering.

Prayers to Jehovah for their disloyalty offered repeatedly for forgiveness and their restoration petitioned daily with the promise of obedience. What "Truth and Consequences" can we learn from this as we apply to what is happening in America.

Covenant Relationship

Every great nation whether they acknowledge or not does not happen without a greater power at work. To understand what brought about this calamity upon Israel, one must first realize that Israel as a nation was in a covenant relationship with God.

A covenant bond usually contains a balanced agreement that both parties are able to keep. The balance between obedience on their part and blessings on God's part complemented each role in the process.

Equally, disobedience on their part and cursing on God's part was proportionately a part of the covenant. Both sides wholly agree to uphold specific aspects of the arrangement as they pertained to each other. This balance was vital to Israel's survival as a nation and a people.

Regrettably, Israel broke the promise by engaging in idol worship and paid a heavy penalty. In the Scripture below, you will discover Israel's confession of failure and guilt, relating to the dilemma that brought about God's punishment. God is always faithful in keeping His promises; however, man will always reap what he sows. What is interesting and should serve as a warning the law of sowing and reaping has never been repealed. The following passage's substantiates these facts.

> *Do not be deceived, God is not mocked; for whatsoever a man sows, that he will also reap* (Galatians 6: 7). *We have become a reproach to our neighbors, a scorn and derision to those who are around us. Oh, do not remember former iniquities against us! Let your tender mercies come speedily to meet us, for we have been brought very low. Help us, O God of our salvation, for the glory of your name; and deliver us, and provide atonement for our sins, for Your name's sake! Restore us, O God; cause Your face to shine, and we shall be saved! O Lord God of hosts, how long will You be angry against the prayer of Your people? You have fed them with the bread of tears, and given them tears to drink in great measure. You have made us a strife to our neighbors, and our enemies laugh among themselves. Restore us, o God of hosts; cause your face to shine, and we shall be saved* (Psalm 79: 4, 8 - 9, 80: 3 – 7)!

Jehovah has not changed only man's perception about God has changed. The same laws and principles apply today as then. True, man can choose his or her life style; they cannot choose the consequences for wrong choices made, no more than Israel could. Punishment for wrong deeds is, reserved, for a sovereign God and God alone.

The Bible teaches that God is the same yesterday, today and tomorrow. He does not need to ask anyone for permission to deal justly concerning sin. Isaiah confirms God's sovereignty in all situations.

> *"You are my witnesses," says the Lord, "And My servant whom I have chosen, That you may know and believe Me, And understand that I am He. Before Me there was no God formed, Nor shall there*

be after Me. I, even I, am the Lord, and besides Me there is no savior"* (Isaiah 43: 10 – 11).

Difficult to Accept

What is difficult for most people to accept is that God will always judge humankind in matters of willful wrongdoing; and never allowed to judge God in reverse concerning His actions. One could argue this is not fair and you would not be the first to raise such an argument.

There is a vast difference between God's absolute justice and man's intended finite system, when it comes to right and wrong as Ezekiel points out.

In the book of Ezekiel, Israel questions God regarding, equality. They accused Him of dealing harshly with them for the sins of their ancestors. They were trying to justify themselves before God on their terms. Sound familiar! God informs them that all souls are His, past, present, and future, and that "His" judgment was impartial.

The Apostle Peter confirms that God's judgment is unbiased and executed according to one's works or deeds. Although the text is lengthy let us review these passages.

> *The word of the Lord came to me again, saying, 'what do you mean when you use this proverb concerning the land of Israel,' saying: 'The fathers have eaten sour grapes, and the children's teeth are set on edge?' As I live, says the Lord God,' you shall no longer use this proverb in Israel. Behold, all souls are Mine; the soul of the father as well as the soul of the son is mine; the soul who sins shall die. But if a man is just and does what is lawful and right; if he has not eaten on the mountains, nor lifted up his eyes to the idols of the house of Israel, nor defiled his neighbor's wife, nor approached a woman during her impurity; if he has not oppressed anyone, but has restored to the debtor his pledge; has robbed no one by violence, but has given his bread to the hungry and covered the naked with*

clothing; if he has not exacted usury nor taken any increase, but has withdrawn his hand from iniquity and executed true judgment between man and man; if he has walked in my statues and kept my judgments faithfully__ he is just; he shall surely live!' Says the Lord God. 'If he begets a son who is a robber or a shedder of blood, who does any of these things and does none of those duties, but has eaten on the mountains or defiled his neighbor's wife; if he has oppressed the poor and needy, robbed by violence, nor restored the pledge, lifted his eyes to the idols, or committed abomination; if he has exacted usury or taken increase shall he then live? He shall not live! If he has done any of these abominations, he shall surely die; His blood shall be upon him. If, however, he begets a son who sees all the sins which his father has done, and considers but does not do likewise; who has not eaten on the mountains, nor lifted his eyes to the idols of the house of Israel, nor defiled his neighbor's wife; has not oppressed anyone, nor withheld a pledge, nor robbed by violence, but has given his bread to the hungry and covered the naked with clothing; who has withdrawn his hand from the poor and not received usury or increase, but has executed My judgments and walked in My statues he shall not die for the iniquity of his father; he shall surely live! As for his father, because he cruelly oppressed, robbed his brother by violence, and did what is not good among his people, behold, he shall die for his iniquity.' Yet you say,' why should the son not bear the guilt of the father? Because the son has done what is lawful and right, and has kept all My statues and observed them, he shall surely live. The soul who sins shall die. The son shall not bear the guilt of the father, nor the father bear the guilt of the son. The righteousness of the righteous shall be upon himself, and the wickedness of the wicked shall be upon himself. But if a wicked man turns from all his sins which he has committed, keeps all My statues, and does what is lawful and right, he shall surely live; he shall not die. None of the transgressions which he has committed shall be remembered against him; because of the righteousness which he has done, he shall live. Do I have any pleasure at all that the wicked should die?' Says the Lord God, 'and not that he should turn from his ways and live? But when a righteous man turns away from his righteousness and commits iniquity, and does according to all the abominations that the wicked man does, shall he live? All the righteousness which he has done shall not be remembered; because of the unfaithfulness of which he is guilty and the sin which he has committed, because of them he shall die.' Yet you say, 'the way of the Lord is not fair. Hear now, O house of Israel, is it not my ways which is fair, and your ways which are not fair? When a righteous man turns away from his righteousness, commits iniquity, and dies in it, it is because of the iniquity which he has done that he dies. Again, when a wicked man turns away from the wickedness which he committed, and does what is lawful and right, he preserves himself alive. Because he considers and turns away from all the he committed, he shall surely live; he shall not transgressions which die. Yet the house of Israel says, the way of the Lord is not fair. O house of Israel, is it not My ways which are fair, and your ways which are not fair? Therefore I will judge you, O house of Israel, every one according to his ways,' says the Lord

> God. *'Repent, and turn from all your transgressions, so that iniquity will not be your ruin. Cast away from you all the transgressions which you have committed, and get yourselves a new heart and a new spirit. For why should you die, O house of Israel? For I have no pleasure in the death of one who dies, says the Lord God. Therefore turn and live* (Ezekiel 18: 1 – 32)! *And if you call on the Father, who without partially judges according to each one's work, conduct yourselves throughout the time of your stay here in fear (1 Peter 1: 17).*

Just as Israel could not escape punishment for wrongful acts as a nation, neither can we. In pure simple language, God set the record straight. There should never be a doubt as to who is in control in matters of right and wrong.

Should one choose to evade these facts, whether an individual or a nation does not alter the truth nor negate the outcome. In light of these truths, let us now turn to what is happening in America and compare the findings.

You may be thinking, "So what! What does that have to do with anything? That was then and this is now." You are not alone thinking this way, and you will find you have a lot of company. This kind of thinking is dangerous, and ignores some basic truths of the Bible.

CHAPTER 1
The Beginning
A Long Journey

America's early beginning was not without hardship and danger as history has recorded. There is an old saying; "A hard beginning makes for a good ending" is not true in every case. The question with reference to a good ending sometimes begs for an answer.

We as a nation currently are searching for this. The intent of this chapter is to draw the reader's attention to our human frailty and consider where we went wrong as a nation.

The testimonial to the "Bread of Tears," found in the Eightieth Psalm, alludes to our chastisement when we fail to obey God's Holy word. The book of Psalms has always been a fascinating tome; and has inspired countless numbers of the human race in their pilgrimage to better understand and cope with the temptations of life.

A Nation is born

1n 1972, I attempted to express my image of our nation in an article "Freedom's Bell" that I composed in simple amateurs terms. I believe I captured in the first sentence "Freedom alone is the soil from which great nations spring" the very sentiments of those who fled their homeland for a new beginning in America. Their desire for freedom outweighed the hardships that awaited their arrival in the new land.

They wanted a new beginning where they and their children could worship freely without suppression by any government, including their own. This was evident by America's first written constitution and signed by the founding fathers of our great land witnessed by the Mayflower Compact 1620.

Forty-One persons signed the compact, and coming to America was not without great risks. As a point of interest, eighteen brought their wives with them twenty-one died the first winter. They selflessly paid a great price for our freedom. It is, believed that twenty-three have descendants now living. Let us review the document as a reminder in history of their sacrifice.

"The Mayflower Compact"

"In the name of God, Amen. We, whose names are underwritten, the Loyal Subjects of our dread Sovereign Lord, King James, by the grace of God, of Great Britain, France and Ireland. King, Defender of the Faith, etc. Having undertaken, for the glory of God, and Advancement of the Christian Faith and the Honor of our King and Country, a voyage to plant the first colony in the northern parts of Virginia; do by these Presents, solemnly and mutually in the Presence of God, and one of another, covenant and combine ourselves together into a civil Body Politick, for our better Ordering and Preservation, and Furtherance of the Ends aforesaid; And by Virtue hereof to enact, constitute and frame, such just and equal Laws, Ordinances, Acts, Constitutions and Offices, from time to time, as shall be thought most meet and convenient for the General good of the Colony; unto which we promise all due Submission and Obedience.

In Witness whereof we have hereunto subscribed our names at Cape Cod the eleventh of November, in the Reign of our Sovereign Lord, King James of England, France and Ireland, the eighteenth, and of Scotland the fifty-fourth. Anno Domini, 1620." *The World Almanac and Book of Facts* 2004 World Almanac Education Group, Pharos Books, New York

Following in Their Footsteps

The succeeding fathers continued in their predecessor's footsteps following those that fought to establish and shape their new homeland. Because of their sacrifices, we have a great heritage to uphold, and should not be taken lightly as many do today. Here is what some of the early defenders had to say to discourage a turning away from those earlier established truths.

William Penn warned those who would engage to do otherwise when he said; "If men will not be governed by God, they will be ruled by tyrants."

Patrick Henry went on to say, "It is when people forget God that tyrants forge their chains." Are we not witnessing this today?

Samuel Adams stated; "He who is void of virtuous attachments in private life is, or very soon will be void of all regard for his country." He went on to say, "There is seldom an instance of a man guilty of betraying his country, who had not before lost the feeling of moral obligations in his private connections." I believe that we all have witnessed the betrayal of this truth by many of our elected officials.

John Adams summed it up by saying; "Our constitution was made only for a moral and religious people. It is wholly inadequate to the government of any other." Meaning, others will not have the same respect or adherence of our constitution and will want to change its originality. This ideology exists today! Last but not least.

Thomas Jefferson the author of our "Declaration of Independence," warned future generations when he wrote; "The Constitution is a mere thing of wax in the hands of the judiciary, which they may twist and shape into any form they please." I believe Jefferson's statement probably carries the most perilous warning and speaks for itself as we have witnessed by some of the laws up help by our Supreme Court.

Imprudent Decision

From the inception of our great nation until the present has not been without challenge or controversy. I do not believe that any one single thing has brought us to where we have deteriorated today; and is the culmination of many wrongful acts over a period-of-time. Example, a major decisive deterioration of our society began when prayer was, taken out of the public school system.

On June 17, 1963, the Supreme Court ruled 8-1, that the "recitation of the Lord's Prayer or Bible verses" in public schools was unconstitutional. This single act of atheism is without a doubt responsible for shaping the future lives of our young people who show little regard for moral values or its principles.

To add insult to injury many believe the removal of prayer was, initiated upon the separation of "Church and State." Many supporters today wish to believe that our founding fathers supported that idea which is untrue.

To validate the constitutionality of separation of "Church and State" the Supreme Court's cites a letter written by Thomas Jefferson. The letter was, written to the Danbury Baptist Association, Danbury, Connecticut allegedly establishing the wall of separation. Nothing could be further from the truth.

In my humble opinion the Supreme Court falsely "cherry picked" the statement made by Thomas Jefferson to the Danbury Association; who respecting their belief that their religious liberties were immutable rights, not privileges established by the State legislature.

The alleged "wall of separation," was to assure the Danbury Association that it was there to protect them from a State established religion, not the other way around.

The constitution makes no, reference to any such law of separation of "Church and State" and actually places the restriction on the government, not the church.

If Benjamin Rush, one of the signers of the "Declaration of Independence," were alive today he would condemn their accusation. He said; "The only means of establishing and perpetuating our Republican form of government is the universal education of our youth in the principles of Christianity by means of the Bible."

This does not sound like separation to me but rather a marriage of Christianity and State without respect to any particular church or denomination.

The Supreme Court decision was in direct opposition to our founding fathers' as seen in the preceding quotes, and only confirms what Thomas Jefferson said; "The Constitution is a mere thing of wax in the hands of the judiciary, which they may twist and shape into any form they please."

Because of this, look what has happened and continues to happen in our school system since one atheist was, allowed to have her way. There has been a steady moral decline and disrespect for spiritual truths or any other since.

The devil could not be happier over that decision by our Supreme Court; and if we could ask him he would probably say; "At last moral influence have begun to crumble and will pave the way for a greater decline." I believe that we are now seeing evidence of this happening all across our land in both the secular and spiritual world.

A Glance into The Past

The past often gives us an insight to what ensues in our future. Looking backward in time, our pathway to failure goes back farther than the example of the Supreme Court decision removing prayer from our schools or the false assumption in the separation of "Church and State." I believe this sort of unjustifiable behavior is, linked to our earlier educational system, which influences every facet of society.

It would appear years ago that people began to outgrow the wisdom of our founding fathers and began to substitute sound doctrine for superficial wisdom. This new age of so-called-discovery and intellect was to be far superior to anything taught in the past. All previous wisdom was now suspect and open to new interpretations and so-called-truths. In support of this view I offer exerts from a newsletter called *The Legal Alert.*

Harvard, one of America's most prestigious colleges founded in 1636, named for its first benefactor John Harvard a young minister. "The governors of the school adopted a seal and motto which was intended (according to Josiah Quincy, president of Harvard in the early Nineteenth Century), to represent the fact that truth was to be found only in the Scriptures, not in words of man's devising."

Later in two separate occasions the motto "Truth" was changed. The motto changed to "In Christi Gloriam" meaning, "In Christ Be Glory." Later changed to, "Christo et Ecclesiae" meaning, "For Christ and church." The changes in the motto were made because of the growing concern by the overseers that Christ "not be removed" from instructions provided by the college.

The leaders saw the value of teaching biblical truths together with secular instructions to maintain equilibrium of the two. It appears that the administrators of Harvard, as did our founding fathers, had their priorities straight. Can we do less and survive?

This concern for truth lasted for over two hundred years of Harvard's history. In 1869, Charles William Eliot took over the school. Eliot was a follower of Charles Darwin who had a brand-new theory involving evolution. According to the article by Dr. Gibbs, "The new president determined that education should involve only truth and not Christ or the church."

This truth was obviously to be, determined by men. "Eliot was unwavering to infuse all teaching at Harvard College with evolutionary philosophies, including teaching in the law." Therefore, man could now define himself as a "Homo Sapiens" meaning learned or wise. Darwin's theory then and now, defies creation as taught in the Bible.

"Eliot and Christopher Columbus Langdell, his newly appointed dean of the law school determined that teaching at the college in all disciplines of education should no longer be focused on God's Word, but on the teachings of men." *The Legal Alert,* by Dr. David C. Gibbs Jr. entitled "Look How Far Our Nations Has Moved," April 2000 edition

A Word to the Wise

We are not the first to fall under the spell of this kind of false intellectual accepted wisdom regardless how presented. The Apostle Paul in his letter to the Corinthian Church warned against those who passed themselves off as the enlightened ones with special wisdom, knowledge, or consciousness.

It has been, said that in Corinth you could meet self-taught sagacious men who mimicked their favorite philosopher by echoing philosophic discussions on any number of topics. They often portrayed themselves as learned or leading authorities in their field of study.

I believe we are seeing a resurrection of such men today spreading their false ideology, both in the church and society. Men today still seek recognition at any cost! Do not be fooled by their cleaver way of twisting the truth.

This so-called special ability was, believed to be "beyond" and not available to the ordinary man, and was usually contrary to the word of God. This tier structure of learning, designed to keep one in their place similar to a caste system. An example of this today is in the term "politically correct."

The idea behind this expression, especially in government, is to get you to line up with those in authority. Surrendering to them their control over you expressed as "dummying down." This is an abandonment of our constitutional rights.

This newfound recognition has no doubt immersed itself into today's beliefs and touted by many called "experts" in their field of academics. I do not wish to imply that people with a higher education are not godly or wise; however, there is a tendency to trust one's own judgment and learning rather than to trust in God's wisdom.

The Bible teaches that the *foolishness of God is wiser than men, and the weakness of God is stronger than men.* For me this separates reality from deception keeping a proper perspective relating to, things that are valid.

> *For the message of the cross is foolishness to those who are perishing, but to us who are being saved it is the power of God. For it is written: I will destroy the wisdom of the wise, and bring to nothing the understanding of the prudent. Where is the wise? Where is the scribe? Where is the disputer of this Age? Has not God made foolish the wisdom of this world? For since, in the wisdom of God, the world through wisdom did not know God, it pleased God through the foolishness of the message preached to save those who believe. For the Jews request a sign,*

and Greeks seek after wisdom; but we preach Christ crucified, to the Jews a stumbling block and to the Greeks foolishness, but to those who are called, both Jews and Greeks, Christ the power of God and the wisdom of God. Because the foolishness of God is wiser than men, and the weakness of God is stronger than men (1 Corinthians 1: 18-25).

Have we reached a point in our society where man's teaching has now become superior to God's and is being touted as the truth, while God's truth has now become suspect or inferior to mans?

It has become easier for many to accept the myth that God's Word is no longer indisputable and open to challenge or useful regarding ones moral behavior. When will humankind recognize that God is supreme and that our existence depends upon Him, and not in the reverse?

The Strong Teacher

Education has always been at the forefront that fuels our nation in producing change. Some changes are for the good while others are bad. This is why a balance between the spiritual and secular it is so important. Harvard's leaders today are vastly different from those leaders of yesteryear when Godly men led the school mentioned earlier.

How you determine good or bad depend upon your perception about one's morals and value system often shaped by society today. This is why we need a moral compass, such as the Bible, to guide us out of the wilderness using reliable truths illustrated by the Ten Commandments.

Learning institutions then and now continue to provide leaders and leadership influencing all facets of our lives. They are not limited to America's politics, religion, law, business, and education. Their influence touches every layer of society from the rank-and-file to the White House.

Knowing this, one does not have to guess what has slowly and continues to take place all across America. All one has to do is turn on the television, pick up a newspaper, or listen to his or her radio and see that America has forgotten the fundamental truths once held by our founding fathers.

True! Harvard cannot be blamed for all of society's ills, other institutions have contributed equally I am sure by following in Harvard's footsteps. All must share in their part of our nation's decline as the results of a conscience decisions made by leaders of yesteryear and today.

The sad commentary is this is a serious reflection on America as a whole, and is an indictment against us that God will not judge lightly. God's judgment is just and sometimes seemingly harsh, but never executed without love. His purpose is to restore those who separated from Him because of sin. Knowing this, what should we do as a nation?

Truth to Live By

Going back to our early existence as a young nation, our leaders recognized the grave importance in the "Truth of God's Word" *And you shall know the truth, and the truth shall make you free* (John 8: 32). They believed the absence of these truths placed them and future generation's freedom in peril.

A departure from these truths would deny them the blessing of God. .Most dictionaries will agree that truth is something that will stand-alone, is self-evident, undeniable, and indisputable as illustrated below

Truth is absolute! Absolute truth does not change over time, nor become non-relevant. I am not saying that truth cannot be, argued against, but I am stating, arguments against the truth will not destroy the self-evidence, the un-deniability, or it being indisputable. Darwin's theory of evolution illustrates this.

There are many claiming his theory to be true, but when new evidence disputing this is presented the proponents have to come-up with something new to keep it alive. Therefore, Darwin's theory does not fit our definition of truth; it is neither self-evident, nor undeniable, or indisputable.

A Biblical example found in Acts 5: 22 – 42. The Apostles were on trial for preaching the Gospel of Jesus Christ. They were, instructed by the High Priests not to teach in the name of Jesus. Peter's reply was, *"We ought to obey God rather than men."* Because of Peter's response, they plotted to kill them.

Then Gamaliel, a teacher of the law well respected by his peers commanded them to release the Apostles. His council to the High Priest was to keep away from the Apostles and leave them alone. His rationale, that if it was the work of men it will come to nothing, but if it is the work of God (meaning truth) you cannot defeat it lest found fighting against God.

No self-respecting Jew would ever knowingly fight against God. The truth of the Apostles teaching continues today. Those whom wish to silence the gospel continues today. Whose side of truth is winning?

Truth is discernible! Truth being so important, is it any wonder that our founding fathers stressed the significance of a Bible based education? The justification of this is, found in the sixth chapter of Deuteronomy.

Moses commands the children of Israel to teach God's statues and judgments lest they forget and enter into a broken relationship and thus forfeit their freedom.

> *Now this is the commandment, and these are the statues and judgments which the Lord your God has commanded to teach you, that you may observe them in the land which you are crossing over to possess, that you may fear the Lord your God, to keep all His statues and His commandments which I command you, you and your son and your grandson, all the days of your life, and that your days may be prolonged. Therefore hear, O Israel, and be careful to observe it, that it may be well with you, and that you may multiply greatly as the Lord God of your fathers has promised you a land flowing with milk and honey. Hear, O Israel: The Lord our God, the Lord is one! You shall love the Lord your God with*

> *all your heart, with all your soul, and with all your strength. And these words which I command you today shall be in your heart. You shall teach them diligently to your children, and shall talk of them when you sit in your house, when you walk by the way, when you lie down, and when you rise up. You shall bind them as a sign on your hand, and they shall be as frontlets between your eyes. You shall write them on the doorposts of your house and on your gates* (Deuteronomy 6: 1 – 9).

The words *you shall teach them diligently to your children,* demands that as parents we have a God given duty to teach our children, about right and wrong pertaining to Godly worship. The responsibility is not, optional, as some might believe. Are we doing this today or are we allowing God's Word to be, replaced by humanism?

Between the sixth chapter and the remainder of Deuteronomy, Moses instructs Israel upon many laws on how to conduct themselves as chosen people to ensure their favor with the Almighty. To be more specific in chapter twenty-eight, Moses pronounces God's' blessings regarding obedience and His curses regarding disobedience.

What is interesting both the blessings and the curses are always meted out in direct proportions to each, occurrence. Israel's blessings were in direct proportion to their obedience to God, and their punishment was equal to their disobedience. God is always just in whatever He does.

Truth is a guide! John Quincy Adams said, "The highest glory of the American revolution was, it connected in one indissoluble bond, the principles of civil government with the principles of Christianity."

It is not hard to see why our ancestors believed that Scriptures, should always, be taught as the supreme guide for our young Republic. Contrary to popular belief, these truths guarantee our freedom and not the loss of it as some think.

Erosion of one's society does not always occur overnight. Sometimes it takes weeks, months, and even years, in some cases hundreds of years for this to happen. All one has to do is look what happened to the Roman Empire.

According to legend the city of Rome founded by Romulus in 753 BC; however, Rome did not emerge as a major power until 500 BC and lasted until about 476 AD.

Despite their accomplishments in civil engineering, the use of cement, water mills, aqueducts, architecture and roads, implies a high standard of living. Their moral climate was idol worship, open homosexuality, violence, and torture that amused the masses at public theaters sanctioned by the state.

Gladiators fought to the death for amusement and look what happened to the Christians during the early church. For spectator sport, fed to the Lions, and burned at the stake to silence them.

Some have compared America to ancient Rome in many aspects. Are we following their example regarding overt homosexuality, moral decay, idol worship, violence, and eventually eliminating all Christian teaching as a way of life?

You may be thinking this can never happen. The daily newscast carries stories of these events happening on a daily basis. Sin is contagious and knows no boundary.

Truth has power to influence! There is a, truth, often overlooked in God's Word that is appropriate in illustrating the power of influence. Influences can be either good or bad. In the book of Matthew, Jesus uses leaven as a symbol for teaching His disciples about this.

Leaven or yeast in the Bible was, and continues in use, to make dough rise. *The kingdom of heaven is like leaven, which a woman took, and hid in three measures of meal, till it was all leavened* (Matthew 13: 33). The keywords, *The kingdom of heaven* is the good influence encompassing the Gospel message spread around the world, which is the good news.

Jesus in that setting again uses leaven to warn His disciples to be aware of the bad influence. *Take heed and beware of the leaven of the Pharisees and the Sadducees* (Matthew 16: 6). The disciples thought Jesus said this because they failed to take bread with them. What He was telling them was to beware of the false doctrine of the Pharisees and Sadducees, and not the fact that they failed to bring bread.

They, like so many today are missing the point. The implication is that our learning experiences and our environment shape and mold our lives while our heredity determines the limits of our intelligence.

In summarization, it is not who we are but what we are taught or not taught that has a direct correlation to what we become, either as a person or a nation for good or evil.

CHAPTER 2

A Nation in Crisis

9 – 11

It would be next to impossible to recount our nation's history from inception until present with any degree of accuracy giving the different interpretation of events reported among newscasters and historians.

I think you will agree we have drifted a long way from our starting point. I will only highlight some of the more recent common events that most can relate that captured America's attention within the last half of the 20th century.

For crisis consideration, this is how I interpret through my lens what has and continues taking place. These events reveal a vital part in describing a "Nation in Turmoil,"

Following the Second World War America was on the industrial move and things could not look brighter. We had won a place in the world as a world leader and power. With this new role came responsibility with certain obligations to other countries. Peace was short lived and we soon found ourselves at war again, this time it was in Korea.

The "50's," aside from the war, began the society of affluence measured by our standard-of-living. This witnessed by two car families, fast food drive inns, outdoor theaters, television, higher education, and the rise of the middle class, etc.

America was enjoying the highest level of comfort that could be experienced anywhere. No doubt, this material comfort was a result in the rise in unionization attributed to our industrial growth, and the government increase in social programs.

In the face of the financially viable success, paralleling this economic growth, the 50's was undergoing a culture shock. Hollywood was mimicking on screen the unruliness that was taking place within society that fueled the flames with movies such as; "The

Wild One and A Streetcar Named Desire" starring Marlon Brando; "Rebel Without a Cause and East of Eden" starring James Dean; and "Blackboard Jungle" starring Glenn Ford, to mention a few.

It was the age of the cool cats, fast cars, greasers, beatniks, drugs, hippies, flower children, and rock and roll music.

Relating to this new unfamiliar culture movement there was concern among many, especially those who came through the great depression and the Second World War it appeared that our culture was going backward.

To add to the worry we were at war in Korea and simultaneously fighting a cold war with Russia that could have escalated into a Third World War at any given moment, and nearly did. Uncertainty was on the increase.

Two Decades Passed

Unlike the 50's, in the 70's, America's confidence in itself was being shaken largely contributed to the Watergate scandal and the Vietnam War. With little moral support from the civilian populace back home, patriotism was at an all-time low witnessed by the treatment of our American Servicemen and Women who were looked, upon with condescension.

The Vietnam War was winding down, and American support for the conflict was losing ground. It was painfully obvious that we were in serious trouble and were not going to win. This would later be seen as a blacken day in our country's history.

Concurrently during this same time, our nation was experiencing difficulty with the identity of its "National Pride," and our role as a "World Leader." There was an ever-growing distrust for our government by the people. We were engaged in a crisis abroad, and at home.

Patriotism was at low ebb draftees were burning their draft cards and fleeing to Canada. Students were protesting on college campuses, in unison with other parts of our land heading toward a national tragedy.

The Kent State shooting took place on May 4, 1970, four students killed and nine wounded while protesting against the war and the draft. Every newspaper, radio, and 6:00 pm television newscast was carrying the story. This unpatriotic behavior displayed at home and abroad was becoming a way of life, unlike any other time in our history.

You get the picture our nation was falling apart. Truly, America was on the move going in the wrong direction. It became painfully clear something had to change to restore patriotism.

A New Start Needed

It was while pasturing a church in Jacksonville, Florida in 1972, where several Navy service members attended my church, and being prior military enabled me to be a better Minister to those in uniform.

I understood what it meant to be away from home apart from loved ones; and what it took to adapt to a new way of life that many civilians could never understand unless they have been there. This close connection helped strengthen my awareness of what was taking place in our country during this time.

As an outreach or extension of ministry, I had the privilege of serving as a Chaplain in the Civil Air Patrol. This extension ministry encompassed supporting our young people who one day may serve in the military.

During that time in an effort to support our men and women in the Armed Forces and regain some of the nation's pride, the "Freedoms Foundation at Valley Forge" sponsored a "Valley Forge Patriots Award." The award was for essays written on the subject "Freedom Has a Price."

This challenge offered to members in the active duty Armed Forces, Reserves, National Guard, and ROTC. I welcomed the opportunity to participate as an Air Force auxiliary member.

The thoughts upon "Freedom" that I pinned over Forty years ago are still in my opinion relevant today. Sadly the sentiments I expressed, are being, eroded because of all the moral decay going on around us. In comparison how I saw our country then and how it is today, is the central argument for my book. Freedom must go beyond mere words, and should be evident in the actions of everyone. As a writer, I have no way to determine what you will think of this particular essay. Perhaps you will agree with it, or you may disagree.

"FREEDOM'S BELL"

"Freedom alone is the soil from which great nation's spring. In the early years of America's history freedom in its pristine beauty is, seen, in the basic principle of this great country, the "Freedom of Worship," which later culminated with the Constitution, and the Declaration of Independence. Since that time until the present it has been unparalleled by any other civilization on earth.

Freedom cannot be, particularized, in static or fragmentary terms. It is neither a liquid, or a solid, or a gas, yet it occupies space. It inhabits space in the hearts and minds of men that believe in it.

Freedom is real, and has a foundation that reaches into infinity. However, it is characterized in numerous ways by many people, and embraces the whole of humanity. To the hungry, it means food; to the thirsty, it means drink; to the depraved, it means salvation; and to the captive, it means release. Unlike the tower of Babel, the tower of freedom will continue as long as men remain unselfish in their challenge to life. Yes! Freedom has a price and that 'Cost' seems basic to every great cause. There is the demand of loyalty, love, pride, patriotism, unselfishness, sacrifice, and the profound respect for the liberty of others.

Every generation is responsible to the next generation so that the freedom now enjoyed is never lost. No other idea conceived seems to penetrate and affect humankind, as freedom does. May we as Christians never rest or cease until its sound and performance has reached around the world, and every man lives under the protection of it." End.

Despite this effort to inspire and influence change, our nation continued to disintegrate on many fronts. We were facing the rise in oil prices. The high cost of government spending on the war was increasing, and a failed attempt to control price increases led to a downturn.

The economy was extremely low; many considered it worse than the great depression, while inflation was at an all-time high reaching nearly twenty-two percent. Overall, the confidence of the people was unbelievably depressing. Things were not looking good for our country as once experienced.

The Brighter Future

In 1984, President Ronald Reagan began a campaign to put America back on-the-right-course as he had promised the American people. In showing my support in his effort I shared with him, two articles I had written earlier as a member of the Civil Air Patrol, which I believed were appropriate.

The second article written in 1982 was in support of our Aerospace program. This initiative was an effort to bring a new awareness, and gain public support, for the program. The article, "Aerospace Established in Strength," which I subtitled "Jachin and Boaz" after the two pillars in Solomon's Temple. Biblically they mean, "He will establish" and "In it is strength."

"AEROSPACE ESTABLISHED IN STRENGTH"
Jachin and Boaz

"For in much wisdom is much grief; and he who increases knowledge, increases sorrow (Ecc.1: 18). This truth comes as an echo out of the past being sounded over and over all across the land, and much of the world today. The present Falkland crisis, the martial rule in Poland, the unrest in the Middle East, civic groups crying out against military buildup, recession and inflation simultaneous at an all-time high, reminds us that we have a tremendous responsibility during these difficult times.

Because our future is, mirrored in our past, we cannot ignore the problems that exist or allow ourselves to accept a lesser role in world leadership involving the military community. The present is not so distance from the past, neither is it so far removed from the future that man at any point along the way can stand and see both directions. Because of this unusual ability, we find ourselves vulnerable and open to defeat while at the same time we strive for peace. The option is ours to pursue the best goals and it is within our power to succeed providing we accept the challenge that has been, thrust upon us.

With each passing day, war camouflaged under the flag of peace by those nations who do not share in our idea of democracy causes us to constantly, evaluate the problems of military strategy, doctrine, leadership, and professionalism within the organization. This has both a positive and negative response within the overall military operation. The positive application is that we cannot allow ourselves to become complacent. One of the best ways to achieve this goal is to become professional in every aspect of the military community. A professional, aviator can be defined as an individual who is highly trained and motivated. He applies his educational knowledge, and technical skill to achieve the highest obtainable goal within the framework and scope of his responsibility. The aerospace program will suffer intensely if we fail to recruit men of such professional caliber.

The idea of professionalism is, sometimes misunderstood, mainly because the professional military man is, thought of as one who thrives on war and war efforts. The aerospace aviator is not to be confused with the former misconception, but expresses a new concept combining learning and technology to stay ahead of the rest of the world. As a result, of this we have become, and remain world leaders in an all-out effort for peace. Our continuing ability to sustain this position depends upon many factors. One of the main factors is the principle of leadership.

There is an ever-increasing demand for superior leadership. Leadership is the by-product of key training, and key training is the product of lengthy research and proven methods. It is like linking the past with the present in order to gain a more meaningful future. Every organization without exception has a problem producing progressive leaders. My definition of a progressive leader is one who is capable of top-level management through new insight within the boundaries of the organization without the loss of purpose. The innovation of a new doctrine or teaching is a solid support in progressive leadership. An anonymous writer has well expressed the close relation between one's belief, activity, character, and destiny in the following: "Sow a thought, reap an act: Sow an act reap a habit; Sow a habit reap a character; Sow a character, reap a destiny."

A man's belief is, so related it cannot help but influence the actions of others. A sound doctrine is necessary for sound influence for a sound aerospace program. In recent years, there has been a tendency to liberalize and even discredit the need of a strong Air Force. Our position is one of strength, and truth. As long as men have knowledge of this, and will apply its principles, we will remain free as a nation.

In order to achieve a greater degree of exactness in stating one's mission, one must develop or review his doctrine of belief. Even though our doctrine tells us what to believe, in an even closer sense "dogma" tell us why we believe. The early pioneers in the aerospace program were men of both strength and character. Any serious airman in order to succeed must possess several characteristics that epitomized their predecessors. First, among the qualifications are, they must have more than an abstract knowledge of aerospace doctrine. They must get personally involved. Second, they must be sincere in their endeavors as an inquirer of truth for the sake of truth. Third, they must possess a trustful spirit that the aerospace program is one of vital importance to the United States and the rest of the world.

Last, but not least is strategy. This is the "how" of the what, who, and why. Without a battle plan, the battle is already lost. In my opinion, more time should be allocated to this area of the overall military operation, than any of the other three that we have covered. As a nation, we have the grave responsibility of insuring world peace. We can have the knowledge and not have the strategy to carry out our mission and we will fail in the end. Our strategy must be precise and accurate down to the last man. There is an old saying, and I believe that it expresses volumes of truth. 'It is not the size of the dog in the fight that counts, but the size of the fight in the dog that determines who wins.'

There are several ideas that support good strategy. First, our motive for engaging the enemy must gain world acceptance. If our motive is right, we will not feel the hostile rebuke of our allies and friends, at home or abroad. Second, our actions must be decisive without waiver in conflict. A well thought battle plan, will result in a well-fought battle. Third, winning must be the supreme objective. We must be willing to go the entire distance. No one will remember a loser, and losers never win.

In summary, the aerospace program has a twofold function. It must provide training for our men and women who have the responsibility to protect our country and much of the world today. Moreover, it must continue to find new ways to achieve and reach new horizons in our changing age. We must remain established in knowledge and strength." End.

I must confess I did not win any prize for either essay. When I wrote those articles, I had no way of knowing they correspondingly would be, shared, with President Reagan's advisors.

On September 27, 1984, I received a letter from President Reagan's Special Assistance and Director of Correspondence, thanking me for my message expressing support for the President's effort to put America-on-the-right-course. I was, notified that my comments were shared with the President's advisors. This was an unexpected honor.

In strengthening our Aerospace program in the 80's was a strong nucleus toward rebuilding our country during, and following the Reagan Administration. The job market began to show signs of gains, and as results of this on the economic front, we were beginning to make substantial gains. Inflation rates began to decline and high interest rates lowered while simultaneously cutting taxes. America was again on the road to recovery or so it seemed.

Paralleling this revival of economic affluence, on the moral front, we were losing the moral fabric of our society that was not a good sign to ensure continued blessings. Hollywood through television and on the big screen was depicting our moral decline influencing direct and indirect participation in immoral activity.

Family values were eroding; the divorce rate was on an incline, and from 1990 to 2001, those who identified themselves as Christians declined by about nine percent depending upon your source.

Too Short Lived

No one could predict what would happen next that literally shocked the world, and has changed our country forever. This was the attack on the World trade center on September 11, 2001. Again, our

Servicemen and Women called upon to answer these acts of war against the United States, deploying troops to Iraq and Afghanistan.

To add to our dilemma there was the growing threat from North Korea and Iran. At present, still at war in spite of everything, our country is trying to dig its way out of a horrible tragedy that no one will ever forget.

Since I started writing this book in 2000, our nation's state of affairs since the 50's are far worse than we could ever imagined nearing epidemic proportions. For instance, newscasts filled with bulletin about public fear, involving the security of our ports and borders; the rising cost of energy; the failed economy; and the political gridlock in Washington.

So far, nothing was working to stimulate the economy, slow the debt, stabilize the housing crisis, strengthen our banking institutions, avoid bankruptcies of failed businesses, and or restart unemployment.

Add to these, the continuing war effort and escalading threat of new wars are of the up-most important concern of the majority of people with little reassurance about the future. Everyone, has questions upon their minds, with little assurance will we survive again?

What People Want Most?

As a society, we are all looking for some sort of balance in our lives to restore our confidence, and ensure our wellbeing. Stability whether as individuals or a nation helps us grow and prosper and reduces stress in our everyday living. Today as witnessed in the 50's many are turning to alcohol and drugs to escape reality rather than to God to achieve this equilibrium.

We now have a drug for about every symptom known to humanity and the legalization of once prohibited drugs are on the rise. I fear that we are fast becoming a drug culture to deal with our problems rather than trust God for our true needs.

To add to this tragedy, depending upon your source, suicides among those between forty-five and sixty have risen thirty percent in the last decade. Consistent with this according to the Center for

Disease Control (CDC), the suicide rate has increased among those born after 1945. There are more than 36,000 suicides annually in the US according to the CDC's 2010 study.

The statistics shows males have a higher rate of suicide, three to four times more likely, than females. Contributing factors: substance abuse, such as alcohol, drugs; mental disorders, such as anxiety, depression associated with change in behavior; medical reasons, chronic pain, cancer, HIV, insomnia, etc...

These events attributed to someone taking their life, can correlate with a spiritual void. Because we are both spiritual and secular beings in this world, it would be unfair to give attention entirely to the secular aspect of our culture and not include the sacred side.

There must be a balance between the religious world and the material world co-existing with each other seeing that God is the God of both. Perhaps we need to reapply some of the old values of our founding fathers to our current problems as a way out.

Good Advice

The primary teaching of Scripture is, directed, toward the spirit of man and his relationship to God. The secondary teaching of the Bible emphasizes our relationship with each other taught in the Ten Commandments. The first Four based upon our association with God. The remaining six has to do with our harmony to each other.

If we fail to keep the first four, then it is impossible to keep the last six. I do not think there is one crime committed that cannot be traced back to the breaking of one of the Ten Commandments. The Commandments are still on God's "Law Books" and are yet to be, repealed.

In fact, Public law 97-280 passed by the Ninety-Seventh Congress of the United States declares the Bible to be the "Word of God" and asks citizens to study and apply the teaching of the Holy Scriptures. This piece of legislature is noble in it 'self, and is to be praised for its intent, but does not go far enough.

When Congress fails to pass laws that compliments and supports this Public law, it becomes little more than window dressing? We cannot allow immorality to flourish and remain moral at the same time, and expect a different outcome from what we are seeing today. The Bible that we are, asked to endorse does not support this kind of logic.

The truth is the Ten Commandments' within itself does not endorse any specific or particular brand of religion. It is, commanded for all humankind the world over without favor. Contrary to what some believe, they do in fact support our judicial system of laws that help govern our nation; therefore making them a historical document. Why we want them removed from public places under force is a mystery to most of us.

The Ten Commandments, (Exodus 20)

I   You shall have no other gods before me.
II   You shall not make for yourself a carved image.
III   You shall not take the name of the Lord your God in vain.
IV   Remember the Sabbath day, to keep it holy.
V   Honor your father and your mother.
VI   You shall not murder.
VII   You shall not commit adultery.
VIII   You shall not steal.
IX   You shall not bear false witness against your neighbor.
X   You shall not covet.

Bringing it Into Focus in The 21st Century

If you agree, the Bible being the most important book once declared by Congress to be the "Word of God." Congress encouraged its citizens to study and apply, begs the question, how do we measure up as a nation?

According to a 2000, Barna survey among people who call themselves Christians, nearly 70 percent said, "That they read the Bible less than twice a week," {this did not include Bible reading at church}, and almost 45 percent said, "they did not read the Bible at all." Is it any wonder that our nation is in a "Catch-22?

Unfortunately, there has been a lot of controversy regarding our nation's problems in the news without any honest attempt by some to report the events as they unfold. Thoughtlessly much of it has been finger pointing across the isles, each political party blaming the other side for the predicament. There is little being done to address the real cause which has brought this tribulation upon our land.

A person or nation cannot separate or dismiss biblical truths from one's daily life without paying the consequences, as we are seeing today because they are, intertwined. God has not left humankind without commands about right and wrong; blessings and cursing; rewards and punishments.

What is happening in our nation is in direct proportion to our rejection of God and our disobedience to the word of God. To believe that one can sin without retribution mocks God.

CHAPTER 3

America vs. Canaan

A Country without God

How does America in the 21st Century compare to a civilization found in the Old Testament? How would you interpret biblical teaching and apply accurately to describe Canaan's behavior reflecting their way of life compared to America. What parallels would you advance to support your claim for impartiality and what yardstick would you use?

To develop impartial, unbiased comparisons are especially difficult when you try to associate a present-day society with one that existed centuries apart.

Typically, with evaluations involving such subject matter one must familiarize themselves with both sides to be able to compare the likelihood of similarities'. At first, the resemblance may seem somewhat obscure giving the era separating the two nations.

Canaan the founding ancestor of the Canaanites portrays a civilization of the past that once knew God, but chose to live outside the parameters that God established for all humanity.

Similar America is a civilization of the present founded upon Christian principles currently choosing to live outside those same parameters. As the subject matter unfolds, it will become undeniably clear there are comparable characteristics between the two societies.

We will discover how God dealt with the descendants of Canaan and why God is bringing judgment upon America as the only logical conclusion.

First Things First

The world as we know it did not pre-exist in any form before God decided to bring it into existence, including the human race. For many this concept is difficult to accept in what we see today at one time never existed before. One must believe in a Creator to establish a fundamental biblical truth that we were, all created, equal in the image of God. *Then God said, 'Let Us make man in Our image, according to Our likeness.' So God created man in His own image; in the image of God He created him; male and female He created them* (Genesis 1: 26a – 27).

Recorded in the book of Genesis simply put, there is God then came humankind. Genesis gives a precise order of the creation process proving that without Him nothing can exist. *In the beginning God created the heavens and the earth* (Genesis 1: 1). *All things were made through Him, and without Him nothing was made that was made* (John 1: 3).

These passages do not imply that God began as if He did not exist before creation, but rather that God is the Creator and origin of all things. God is autonomous over everything within this vast cosmic universe including the supreme right of judgment over everything that He created.

Our Creator is absolute not dependent upon man for His existence, His contentment, or His wellbeing. God is self-reliant, self-contained, and is not dependent upon anything created. A truth often overlooked man on the other hand must rely wholly upon God for all of his needs. Everything that man has is on loan from His Creator. Therefore, he cannot claim any ownership over it, only his stewardship as the Lord relinquishes it to him.

> *Then God blessed them, and God said to them, 'Be fruitful and multiply; fill the earth and subdue it; have dominion over the fish of the sea, over the birds of the air, and over every living thing that moves on the earth* (Genesis 1: 28).

God blessing Adam and Eve means that God provided all the resources necessary for them to have communion and maintain a spiritual union with Him providing they obeyed His commandments. This harmony was crucial in keeping companionship with God, and avoiding punishment, as Adam and future generations were to discover.

A Journey from God

From Adam until the flood was approximately eleven hundred and fifty six years. During that period, Adam's off spring began to forget God, and do evil wicked things in His sight with no regard for Him. The wickedness of man was increasing until the whole earth was corrupt.

Because God's nature cannot tolerate sin, their behavior displeased the Lord very much causing Him to destroy the earth and its inhabitants with the exception of Noah and his family.

> *Then the Lord saw that the wickedness of man was great in the earth, and that every intent of the thoughts of his heart was only evil continually. And the Lord was sorry that He had made man on the earth, and He was grieved in His heart. So the Lord said, 'I will destroy man whom I have created from the face of the earth, both man and beast, creeping thing and birds of the air, for I am sorry that I have made them.' But Noah found grace in the eyes of the Lord* (Genesis 6: 5 – 8).

Initially upon reading, these passages become difficult to interpret without what some scholars refer to as the "accommodation theory," which helps us understand God's actions in response to something. This makes possible for the human mind to understand difficult Scriptures that relates to the infinite qualities of God.

God being sorry He made man {some translations use "repented"}, and was grieved in His heart is not to be confused. God wanting to destroy humankind is not easy to understand. God is not apologizing to man as some might think. He was sorry that He made man because of their wickedness. One more truth that cannot be ignored has to do with man's' failed purpose over what God had planned for him.

The term *I will destroy* is a solemn warning to those who try to defeat, resist, or reject God's purpose in their life. They will have no claim or permanent title to eternal life while in a state of rebellion. Those destroyed were those who rejected God, and resisted His love after given one-hundred twenty years to repent while Noah built the Ark as God commanded. While salvation is in obedience to God's, word there is nothing we can do to earn our way to heaven. It is God's gift on His terms.

Noah Found Grace

If Noah had followed the crowd, humankind as we know it today would not exist because all life would have ended with the flood. All previous souls would perish because Christ could not have been born. *Noah found grace in the eyes of the Lord* is more than a song or Bible verse we learned as a child.

Escaping the flood only eight righteous people remained alive. They were Noah, his wife, their three sons, Shem, Ham, Japheth, and their three-wives. This conveys a deliverance from death for the righteous, and shows evidence of God's love and mercy to those who repent. His mercy is still, extended today to those who accept Jesus on God's terms.

Canaan is born

To compare America with Canaan, we need to understand how the Canaanites came about. To do this we need to look at the rest of the account following the flood. There are several events that occurred in Noah's household, that are necessary to the narrative.

The Scriptures tells us in Genesis chapter nine following the flood, Noah planted a vineyard where he drank of the vine, became drunk lying uncovered in his tent.

Ham seeing the nakedness of his father that was forbidden and told his two brothers who refused to look upon their father's bareness, chose to cover Noah with a covering. Here is an example of good and evil at work, the wrong seen in the actions of Ham, and the good performed by the two brothers.

Because of Ham's disregard for his father, when Noah awoke from his inebriated state and learned what the younger son had done unto him, he said: *Cursed be Canaan; A servant of servants he shall be to his brethren* (Genesis 9: 25). According to Jewish Scholars in ancient times any blessing or curse given by the father, was believed to affect the latter's descendants. In this situation, it affected Ham's son Canaan who became the father of the Canaanites.

It should, be noted that the curse was not immediate, and was later fulfilled upon the Canaanites because of their misconduct before the Lord. Their wickedness was not the effect of the curse as if Noah cast a spell upon them, as some might believe, but rather the curse because of their iniquity. God foresaw the path that Canaan would chose and exercised the right to punish as promised.

Like Canaan, we can trace our roots back to Noah, and Noah's back to Adam. This is representative having come from the same ancestry. Henceforth we are capable of committing the same wrongs as our ancestors.

We in a sense are all brothers of split branches of the first family. Knowing this, one would think there would be a greater effort to preserve the family, live in harmony, and not destroy it as seen in Noah's day and what we are seeing today.

If the Bible makes anything clear, it is clear about the home. The institution and relationship or union between a man and a woman is sacred before God. The family and its values, is the bond to any society. Without the home intact, our civilization would fall apart. This was true for Canaan and is true for America.

As a point of interest before we leave this segment, some scholars believe that Noah being the first to cultivate the vine did not know of the intoxicating nature of the wine, and his getting drunk was unintentional. Whether that explanation is true or not, to my knowledge, there is never a mention of this happening again in the life of Noah.

If shame and evil through drunkenness can degrade a person like Noah who otherwise found righteous and blameless before God, should serve as a warning against strong drink. The evidence is clear about what it can do to a person's respectability and effect it has upon the family.

Set of Laws to Live By

According to Jewish teachings the verses found in Genesis chapter nine expressing the covenant between God and Noah, established seven moral/judicial systems of laws for this new civilization to live by. They articulated a non-discriminating means to settle disputes, live in harmony, and obey God.

The laws forbid blasphemy, idol worship, incest, stealing, the shedding of blood, and dietary laws involving animal blood. Whether Canaan or America, in any society, humanity needs sound principles of conduct, which are paramount to protect and serve its members.

Because Canaan failed to live by these laws, we are, given insight into the relation of cause and effect for the crime committed. *Do not be deceived, God is not mocked; for whatever a man sows, that he will also reap* (Galatians 6: 7). Obedience then is greater than sacrifice.

Lawless acts carry severe consequences that are not always evident at the time committed. Example, in the first family of Adam and Eve, Cain killed Abel. If humankind had adopted these laws as God intended and allowed them to govern as a guide, it is conceivable that in the second family bloodshed would be outdated.

All Humankind has a responsibility to live morally before God as God intended. To live contrary to this brings about God's judgment and wrath upon those who fail to be obedient as seen in Paul's letter to the Romans. *But in accordance with your hardness and your impenitent heart you are treasuring up for yourself wrath in the day of wrath and revelation of the righteous judgment of God, who will render to each one according to his deeds* (Romans 2: 5 – 6).

Leaving one's Sacred Heritage Behind

Several generations,' passes the world again has grown wicked and began to worship other gods as did the generations of Adam before them. The farther they went from their Creator the more real their gods became, until finally they could worship them without their conscience bothering them.

Humankind, "namely the Canaanites," was on a downward spiral without any brakes. The practice of paganism was at its highest apex with little or no regard to life or morality.

A prime example of this form of pagan worship was the worship of other gods such as Moloch. This form of worship caused their children to pass through the fire in sacrifice to their heathen god. Comparably does abortion come to mind?

This disregard to human life is in direct disobedience to God's Word. This custom of worship placed them in direct conflict with God's blessings and instructions to both Adam's and Noah's descendants to be fruitful and multiply.

The Canaanites passed National Laws that endorsed their worship of idols, and the pagan rituals practiced by the people. Canaanite laws had now replaced God's law and regarded to be superior in the sense they believed to be reciprocal.

In essence, they worshipped to please their idols or gods and in return, the idols were to bless them. The more bazaar the worship the more their gods would bless them, or so they thought. These practices were in direct conflict with divine teaching and were, prohibited, by God for the children of Israel to practice.

Forms of Pagan Worship

Let us examine some of the forms-of-worship the Canaanites performed that God has instructed His chosen people not to follow.

> *Then the Lord spoke to Moses saying, "Speak to the children of Israel, and say to them; I am the Lord your God. According to the doings of the land of Egypt, where you dwell, you shall not do; and according to the doings of the land of Canaan, where I am bringing you, you shall not do; nor shall you walk in their ordinances. You shall observe My judgments and keep My ordinances, to walk in them; I am the Lord your God. None of you shall approach anyone who is near of kin to him, to*

uncover his nakedness: I am the Lord" (Leviticus 18: 1 - 4, 6).

Canaanite pagans engaged in marriages to near blood relations, this practice was, forbidden, by God for the children of Israel.

The term *uncover his nakedness* has to do with one's marriage to their near blood kin such as mother, father, sister, brother, son, daughter, aunt, uncle, sister-in-law, brother-in-law, daughter-in-law, son-in-law, granddaughter or grandson to mention a few.

Any, union between these groups are, considered incestuous and forbidden. These incestuous unions practiced by the Canaanites reported in America as well.

Other practices by the pagans that God forbid the Israelites to have anything to do with they were forbidden, to commit adultery; they were forbidden same sex sexual relations, deemed as abominable before God; and any sexual relations in any form with animals are forbidden to either man or woman. The latter act is, seen as perversion in its worst form.

Moreover, the pagans went so far as to have temple prostitutes. They substituted the truth for a lie and were boastful about it. They, were given over to the craving of sheer pleasure absent from the consciousness of the mind, as to one's identity or purpose in life. Sound familiar!

In Deuteronomy Moses, further spells out certain wicked customs the Canaanites practiced and warns them that God has not appointed such for them.

> *When you come into the land which the Lord your God is giving you, you shall not learn to follow the abominations* (or detestable acts) *of those nations. There shall not be found among you anyone who makes his son or his daughter pass through the fire,* (or be burned as an offering to an idol) *or one who practices witchcraft, or a soothsayer, or one who interprets omens, or a sorcerer, or one who conjures spells, or a medium, or a spiritist, or one who calls up the dead. For all who do these things are an*

abomination (or detestable) *to the Lord, and because of these abominations the Lord your God drives them out from before you* (Deuteronomy 18: 9 – 12).

Additional insight of pagan conduct can be, found in the remainder of chapter's eighteen, nineteen, and twenty. These three chapters can be, summarized as moral breakdown, moral renewal, and punishment. I strongly encourage you to read these chapters.

Chapter nineteen deals with God's instructions to His people in the way they are to conduct themselves. Moreover, in chapter twenty, we see the penalties or punishment ascribed for breaking God's law. God in His wisdom, love, and compassion instructs Moses to warn the children of Israel.

Understanding what God warned Israel about with reference to faithfulness involving moral living leaves little doubt how a nation is to conduct their affairs. When an individual or nation forgets God, they begin to substitute other avenues for their spiritual guidance usually associated with false conviction.

Often they turn to drugs, alcohol, seek out fortune-tellers, wizards or tarot readers, in search of happiness and assurance. To live in accord to God's Word guarantees God's blessings and assurance, to live contrary to His Word will deserve His wrath.

Like Canaan like America

One can hardly deny there are many similarities between America and the Canaanites of old. How do we as America, compare to all of this so far? Reminiscent of the Canaanites many of our National Laws oppose God's laws by supporting immoral practices as an acceptable way of life, including abortion, homosexuality, same sex marriages and other provocative practices.

Unless there is a turning back the clock, I predict that in time the "state" will become uncharitable of any religion or people of conscience. The handwriting is already on the wall.

Depending upon your source, more than twenty-five percent polled believe in clairvoyance and more than thirty percent believe in telepathy or psychic communications. Psychic phenomena in all its forms tarot readers, clairvoyants, spiritualist, psychic mediums, and horoscopes to mention a few; has become a way of life to knowing the future.

Something that is equally disturbing, there have never been a time in history where we have so many celebrity types that people actually worship. We may not bow down to these idols as the pagans of old, but we are just as enslaved and committed to follow their so-called enlightenment and mimic their behavior regardless of how bazaar.

They have become idols and mini gods to the masses {they have become our god Moloch}. This was, recently observed when Michael Jackson passed away.

The social and religious climate among many today, live only for fleshly pleasure and is unambiguously described in Paul's letter to the Romans. Although Paul was writing for his day, it is equally applicable today.

> *For the wrath of God is revealed from heaven against all ungodliness and unrighteousness of men, who suppress the truth in unrighteousness, because what may be known of God is manifest in them, for God has shown it to them. For since the creation of the world His invisible attributes are clearly seen, being understood by the things that are made, even His eternal power and Godhead, so that they are without excuse, because, although they knew God, they did not glorify Him as God, nor were thankful, but became futile in their thoughts, and their foolish hearts were darkened. Professing to be wise, they became fools, and changed the glory of the incorruptible God into an image made like corruptible man and birds, and four-footed animals and creeping things. Therefore God also gave them up to uncleanness, in the lusts of their hearts, to dishonor their bodies among themselves, who exchanged the truth of God for the lie, and worshipped and served the creature rather than the*

Creator, who is blessed forever Amen. For this reason God gave them up to vile passions. For even their women exchanged the natural use for what is against nature. Likewise also the men, leaving the natural use of the woman, burned in their lusts for one another, men with men committing what is shameful, and receiving in themselves the penalty of their error which was due. And even as they did not like to retain God in their knowledge, God gave them over to a debased mind, to do those things which are not fitting (Romans 1: 18 – 28).

We now worship the creature more than we do the Creator. Sexual conduct is out-of-control including perversion with animals. Both pre-marital and extra marital sex is all too commonplace among the masses. Adultery has become all too frequent among many married couples. Sensual material such as pornographic literature, adult X rated movies and exploiting children is in big demand portraying children as adults.

This so- called adult, entertainment, sanctioned by the so-called, "freedom of speech advocates" would have you believe this type of freedom is guaranteed by our constitution.

As a result, same sex life styles and same sex marriages are gaining support and no longer looked upon as being wrong by many today. All one has to do is turn on their television to witness a life style that has gone astray. We are in grave danger of losing the family the nucleus that makes up our society.

Before I forget, we are witnessing an upsurge in violence and unthinkable heartless behavior. Between 1991 and 2011, in just five incidents involving shootings eighty-seven people were, killed and eighty-six wounded not including the shooters who committed suicide.

These crimes are now being committed by our younger generation, who years ago with few exceptions would never engage in such practices. The trouble our nation is experiencing today is directly, related to our immoral behavior, and can only get worse if we continue down this same road.

Seek and You Shall Find

You may be asking; "Is there a way out of this quagmire we have gotten into?" In order to answer this, it is important to understand the separation of Israel as a nation from their heathen neighbors the Canaanites.

In the book of Leviticus, the first half of the book applies to sacrifices ordained by God, and His laws banishing magic, incantations, idolatry, and child sacrifices. The second part of the book has to do with sanctification or set apart of human life, for worshipping *God in Holiness.*

The term Holiness is, embedded in one's thoughts and actions of one's daily routine. Israel could no longer practice immorality as the nations around them and worship a holy God at the same time, neither can we.

The bases of Israel's newfound spiritual practices has more to do with repentance, restitution, and separation in order to be free from immoral behavior, rather than defiled ceremonially as the heathen tribes around them.

Like, Israel America must separate our self from immoral conduct as a nation, and return to its moral values that we once knew in days past, or suffer the consequences.

Before we leave this chapter, it is crucial to understand what happened to the Canaanites beginning with the city of Jericho whose cup of transgressions was full. In the book of Joshua, God commands Joshua to cross over Jordan into Canaan, to possess the land that He promised there ancestor's.

What is interesting Jericho had forty years to repent of their pagan ways while the children of Israel wandered in the wilderness after leaving Egypt. They knew that God had given Israel their land and faced destruction because of their depraved wickedness, yet they did not repent.

What makes this difficult to understand, the Scriptures tells us that forty years earlier they heard how God had dried up the Red Sea when

Israel came out of Egypt. Moreover, what God did to the two kings of the Amorites, Sihon and Og whom they destroyed.

Because of what they heard, the people of Jericho heart has melted with fear; neither were there any more courage in them because of Israel's Lord, whom they declared to be God in heaven above and on the earth below Joshua 1: 2. This should have served as a warning!

Before one jumps to conclusions and reaches an unfair opinion about God relating to the Canaanites being destroyed. God will not tolerate sin indefinitely and there becomes a point when sin must be, punished. They were, destroyed, for their atrocious events involving human sacrifices and their blatant immorality.

God was not befriending the Israelites at the expense of the Canaanites as some might think. God made a decision against sin and iniquity for righteousness sake. Israel was under the same judgment in the event they practiced the same flagrant rituals as the heathens around them as are we Leviticus 18: 24-29.

Consequently, America's cup is nearing becoming full. Should we not fear the same judgment?

CHAPTER 4

Abortion

America's Holocaust

Abortion, America's holocaust, is a national tragedy unlike any other in our nation's history. Life is our most precious possession and should be, guarded against the willful destruction against its existence.

Loss of life under any circumstance is terrible and our evening news carries stories of unlawful deaths every day, some more horrendous that others. I will devote this chapter to its topic and untainted truths and reserve judgment for chapter five.

As I am writing this manuscript, the news is carrying the story of what just occurred at Virginia Tech. The final count was thirty-two students lost their lives and seventeen wounded in a bizarre shooting that involved a fellow student. Details concerning this tragedy are still coming in, and will be the subject of debate for a long time to come.

An earlier incident that caught everyone's attention was the fatal shooting at Columbine High in 1999, claiming twelve lives and injuring twenty-one students. Heartbreaks such as these should have never happened.

Caught off Guard

What happened at the Columbine High School in Colorado and VA Tech, underlines the acceleration in the moral collapse in our land. When aired on television, all across America felt the pain. We were asking ourselves, "What is happening to everyone, how could such a catastrophe happen; how could young people shoot down their own peers in cold blood?"

Add to the list the latest tragedy, the shooting at Sandy Hook, taking twenty lives of our young children and adults. The question "Why," continues to be on the minds of people everywhere with seemingly no tangible answer in sight. Perhaps we are looking in the wrong place and need to look elsewhere for the cause.

Could it be possibly those responsible may never have heard of the sixth commandment, *You shall not kill*? Had the Ten Commandments remained posted in their school there would have been a daily reminder of right verses wrong. Without our moral compass and guide we all can become lost as those youths were who did those dreadful deeds.

In my opinion Columbine, was the tip-of-the-iceberg portraying a nation, gone crazy. Unfortunately, many times the innocent suffer because of a mistake in judgment made by others leading to wrong decisions. Who then is to blame and is it fair to ask?

An interrelated possibility, undeniable with certainty, what happened at Columbine, Virginia Tech or Sandy Hook related to the granting of abortion. The abortion issue has been around a long time planting the idea that life is cheap. True! What can a nation expect when one's conscience grows dull concerning the value of life after having denounced God for all practical purposes?

America's Holocaust

Just short of Ten years after removing prayer and Bible reading from public schools. The Supreme Court on January 22, 1973, in a seven to two vote ruled that a state must not prevent a woman from having an abortion during the first six months of her pregnancy.

This later expanded to include partial birth abortions and some even proposing expanding the limits. This carnage upon our nation against the unborn has "no equal" in the world. The worst condemnation against America like Canaan is the sacrifice of human life.

In Canaan, they caused their children to pass through the fire in worship of their god "Moloch." In America, we abort the unborn in worship of our god "Women's Rights." As you read this chapter, keep chapter three, "America vs. Canaan," in mind. It will keep all this in its right perspective.

We See In a Mirror Dimly

For those who wonder about what happens to the innocent babies who are aborted. I asked God on different occasions during my prayer time, "Why do you allow this to happen?" The long awaited reply came back indelibly pressed upon my mind that I could not shake; "I am filling my Kingdom."

I believe the Bible teaches that God has two discernible wills that distinguishes His actions from all others. First, there is His active will where He intervenes, or He is the direct cause of something to happen that defies human reason.

Second, His permissive will where He allows tragedies to happen, such as tornados, earth quakes, floods, and even abortion though He could have prevented should He desired

I have to admit beyond this my understanding is limited, and God does not have to give an account to man why He allows or does not allow certain things to happen. Sin left unchallenged knows no limits including the conscience ability to murder one's own unborn.

I believe that His mercy and love for the aborted having been unwanted and unloved by their parents understood in the book of Psalms. *For He shall give his angels charge over you, To keep you in all your ways. In their hands they shall bear you up, Lest you dash your foot against a stone* (Psalms 91: 11 – 12).

The implication here reflects His care and love for the innocent in this life and beyond. When it becomes necessary they meaning angles, as a nurse would care for the sick, will carry them upward. I know that God is just and the record will be set straight concerning all these matters involving immoral choices someday.

This being true, I need to add, the acts of those who perform abortion are never justified, and stands condemned before God even though the law allows.

> *For we know Him who said, 'vengeance is mine, I will repay,' says the Lord. And again, the Lord will judge His people. It is a fearful thing to fall into the hands of the living God* (Hebrews. 10: 30 – 31).

Because judgment does not come immediately to the guilty does not nullify God's justice or limit His mercy. He is giving the guilty time to repent before standing before His judgment seat. Our prayer is that they will take the only opportunity offered to them in this lifetime and seek His forgiveness.

Is Our Silence Golden?

There is a familiar Scripture found in the Old Testament often overlooked, that foretells of Jesus entry into Jerusalem which prophesizes the praise of the people that is to be, bestowed upon Him. The Gospel of Luke gives us the actual account prophesized by Zechariah of Jesus' making His "Triumphal Entry" into Jerusalem to celebrate the Passover.

> *Rejoice greatly, O daughter of Zion! Shout, O daughter of Jerusalem! Behold, your King is coming to you; He is just and having salvation, lowly and riding on a donkey, A colt, the foal of a donkey* (Zechariah 9: 9).

Upon entering the city, the crowd begins to praise Him. The Pharisees call to Him and ask, "That He rebuke His disciples." Jesus replies: *I tell you that if these should keep silent, the stones would immediately cry out* (Luke 19: 40). Has the church been silent too long on sin?

Most biblical scholars agree that Scriptures primarily have one predominant exegesis. In addition, they may have other spiritual applications related to their principle teaching.

In re-reading this to discover its intended truth, I believe the fundamental interpretation is, had the people not shouted with joy and praise in fulfilling this prophecy acknowledging Christ as Lord of lords and King of kings, the stones would have literally miraculously cried out in their place.

Could it be then, that we have been silent too long must the rocks cry out? Are we becoming too complacent about speaking out against sin in any form flaunted by our society today? Is our silence affecting our relationship with God?

In parallel I ask you; "could it be then that God is filling His kingdom with the innocent that are being aborted, because modern man refuses to repent of his sins saying, "I am god I have no need to repent?"

Opposite Sides of the Coin

Like many subjects, there will always be debate among people and one side will usually decide to choose against the other depending upon what they believe. In a number of groups, each seeks the approval of someone noteworthy to indorse their position on the matter right or wrong. The position chosen carries a lot of influence.

An example of this, Jesus questioned about the lawfulness of paying taxes to Caesar. His answer was to be the tipping point of betrayal or so they thought. Knowing their craftiness He asked for a coin and inquired about whose inscription was on the coin. Then He made an upsetting statement, replying they were to render equally to both, Caesar and God, that which belongs to each Luke 20: 20 – 25.

Unlike the Pharisees, who wanted it their way, truth can only be found when people are willing to lay aside their pride, prejudices, selfishness, and arrogance. The Bible contains His Word, which cannot be, judged by the human race, nonetheless will be used to judge all humankind. One must be willing to seek truth by going back to its' original source which brings the next point.

To choose or not to choose Abortion, who is right and who is wrong? Is it the pro-choice, or the pro-life group? Both sides stand for choice involving life and death. Each side uses persuasive arguments to support their claims for acceptance or rejection by the populace. Thus, the struggle continues and each group grows further apart in resolving the issue of abortion.

In the meantime, over one million plus babies aborted each year in the United States, and the count grows. Regardless of which side you choose, I am pro-life; I think it is time to set the record straight concerning what constitutes life and its eternal consequences.

As of January 2014, it is reported over fifty six million abortions have been performed in our country alone since 1973. This is nine times more than, all the Jewish people killed in the holocaust or ten times the population of Minnesota.

Let us examine abortion from two different perspectives; first, from the aborted fetus and second, from Gods? Caution must be, taken when placing oneself above the word of God. It is here that I believe the real problem lies.

The Silent Minority without a Voice

There is a word used in our court system that implies that another can speak for someone who is incapable of speaking on, their own behalf. That term is *"guardian ad litem."* As that spokesperson' I will speak for all the unborn aborted babies from their perspective bearing in mind they cannot speak for themselves. I do this with God's permission.

My name is not important I am an unborn infant; I never received a birth certificate to prove I ever existed. There will be no monument to mark my grave. Here is how it all began. Life for me began at conception, and from that moment, I began to grow in my mother's womb. It was here that I felt warm and safe. After several weeks, I could suck my thumb; I could kick, yawn, and stretch; I dreamed of the day when I would be born.

I could hear sounds coming from the outside. I wondered, was it the voice of my mom and dad? I looked forward with great joy to seeing my parents; to be able to sit in their lap; to have them hold me, and sing lullabies to me. I wanted to see my grandparents, my aunts and uncles, go to school, and one day get married and have a family of my own. I believed this to be my destiny in life.

Suddenly without warning, all that changed! A horrible thing happened. I felt the burning pain from some awful solution. I felt my bones being broken and my limbs torn from my body as if I were not human and felt no pain. I cried___ and cried___ as hard as I could, but they would not stop.

I ask why this is happening; no answer came. I thought what evil person could do this and take the life of an unborn baby. The torturous pain was so great I could no longer bear it. Within minutes, the agony overcame my body then it was over, an angel came and carried me to my Heavenly Father.

When I got to heaven, I asked my Father, "Did you hear my cry for help?" My Father comforting me said, "My child I heard your cry, saw your tears, and hear all the cries of the unborn that are aborted. Dry your tears come and see what I have prepared for you. Afterward I will tell you a story of how it all began many, many years ago, then you will better understand how this could happen."

From Beauty to Ashes

There is another word in Latin "Sacerdos," meaning one who presents to God, as in prayer, and one who speaks for God on His behalf. It is the later that I will do; and again I believe with God's permission.

God said; "Listen carefully my child it all started in the Garden-of-Eden. The garden was one of my most beautiful creations in nature. I created it especially for Adam and Eve, whom I created to have communion with me. I made them in my own image of holiness and righteousness. They were faultless without sin. In the garden, I provided everything for their joy and happiness, there was nothing they lacked.

I gave them only one commandment to keep. They were free to wander taking anything in the garden with-one exclusion. They could enjoy everything with the exception of the fruit from one tree in the midst of the garden. They were free to obey my command or they could break my word and suffer the consequences of their choice.

One day Eve was walking past the tree with the forbidden fruit, and the old serpent (Satan) tempted Eve to eat of the fruit. Lucifer attempting to mock God, told Eve that what God had told her and Adam was not true. Being, taken in by all the devil had said, she ate the fruit and then gave to Adam.

This is how sin entered the human race. From that day forward, humankind has sinned and chooses control over their life.

In the absence of moral guidance immoral practices flourish. They do not want to acknowledge that I am God, nor do they obey my word; and they behave like their father the devil.

This is why, laws, can be passed and those who sit in judgment can ignore the moral commandments of God, replacing them with their own statutes that serves their sinful interests. This is why horrible acts such as abortion, can be done without shame, because they see themselves as god."

"What will happen to them Father," asked the child? To this God replied; "just as Adam and Eve elected not to keep my word in the Garden-of-Eden, and later repented, they must also choose to repent from this evil and obey my word.

Unless they repent and ask forgiveness for the wrongs they have committed, and turn from their wicked way they will be cast into outer darkness with their father the devil for eternity. For their salvation, every provision provided through Jesus Christ My only Son. I do not wish that any should perish, the choice is theirs to make."

False Truths Lead to False Assumptions

There are several misconceptions peddled as truth by the Pro-Choice group that many have bought into needing to be exposed. The first misconception it is my body and I can do with it whatever I want. Perhaps this deception accounts for one and three women having an abortion before they reach their mid-forties of age.

The second misconception is that life begins at birth, not at the time of conception; therefore, concluding aborting the fetus prior to normal birth does not constitute the taking of a life. How convenient to sooth our conscience to commit murder.

Let us begin with the false impression "It is my body, I can do whatever I want." This concept of one being independent and not held accountable is not justified in truth. Eve, meaning *life or living* long ago demonstrated that same attitude only under a different circumstance. The Bible is plain regarding the reality surrounding the deception of Eve by the devil as shown by her attitude representative of independence and disregard of truth found in Genesis 2: 16 - 17, 3: 1 – 5.

Just as Eve, was deceived by Satan in the Garden-of-Eden women all across the world are being equally deceived by the notion it is their body. Eve, like her adversary the devil, wanted to exert herself and be like God. Many have stepped outside the bounds for which they were created, and have taken upon themselves the role of a god.

This kind of behavior can only end in tragedy. True, you could say that Satan tricked Eve, but that does not discount or excuse her from her actions.

Here is something to think about, I suspect that Satan is willing to wager, knowing that an aborted infant will go to heaven, at the risk of those responsible will not repent, and he gets them in the end.

Created in God's Image

The second misconception is "Life begins at birth" not at conception, which they consider a mass of tissue. For us to appreciate life, and how we connect to one another, each human being begins as a single cell. This single cell is the results of the fusion of two cells, one from the mother and the other from the father. The cell then divides into two; these two divide into four; these four divide into eight, and so on until the infant is developed.

The time lapse between the first single cell division in the womb and the last cell division to create this whole person is crucial. Life is not a game! There is a fallacy that some believe time is a major factor in the birth process that determines when life begins.

In support of this assumption, some have determined that anything between conception and full term is fair game, no matter how you play. This false so-called truth supports their rationale for abortion.

Any planned outside interference of development such as abortion should carry the penalty of first-degree murder. The biblical truth of the development is that life begins at conception not at full term birth, as abortion advocates would have you believe.

Because time is primarily associated to man's activities, and does not govern God or God's blueprint when it comes to life. This is not to say that God does not have a plan nor that time is not important to Him. It is that we view time differently and for different reasons.

Example, if a child dies moments after conception, or lives to a ripe-old-age is inconsequential. Our length of time on earth in our earthly body has no bearing on what our eternal heavenly body will be like; time is not a factor in this.

From the moment of conception, all the provisions been provided by our Creator that are necessary for an embryo to become a whole person. There is additional biblical proof that life begins at conception and that God's role is paramount in the process. This is seen in Jeremiah and Psalms when God spoke to Jeremiah about his birth and David confirms' God's perfect knowledge of man.

> *Then the word of the Lord came unto me saying: "Before I formed you in the womb I knew you; Before you were born I sanctified you; I ordained you a prophet to the nations"* (Jeremiah 1: 4 – 5).
> *For You formed my inward parts; You covered me in my mother's womb. I will praise You, for I am fearfully and wonderfully made; Marvelous are Your works, And that my soul knows very well* (Psalms 139:13 – 14).

The Psalmist David further spoke of his birth in similar language acknowledging his carnal nature that he was born with from the moment of conception. *Behold, I was brought forth in iniquity, and in sin my mother conceived me* (Psalm 51: 5).

If David was not a human being at conception then how could he have been born with a sin nature? It would be impossible. In proceeding versus David confesses his sin to God as the results of his nature he was born with.

He acknowledged his transgressions as his, and judged God to be, just and blameless in the whole process. In fact, "Without God" no life would exist past, present or future.

Consequences of Abortion

The Bible gives a strong warning to those found guilty who have consented to have an abortion and those who perform the act of abortion. The Old Testament gives detailed instructions for the protection of a woman during pregnancy and the penalty paid if she gives birth prematurely due to any harm to her. Care was to be, taken not to do injury to her and cause her to lose the fruit of her womb. To do so was a punishable offense.

> *If men fight* (or struggle), *and hurt a woman with child, so that she gives birth prematurely, yet no harm follows, he shall surely be punished accordingly as the woman's husband imposes on him; and he shall pay as the judges determine. But if any harm follows, then you shall give life for life* (Exodus 21: 22 – 23).

God's Word is clear on the subject and answers the question, how could a woman give birth prematurely if life does not exist in the womb? This proves beyond doubt that life begins at conception, and willful destruction invokes God's punishment.

God Has a Plan

God has chosen that the union between a man and a woman, whereby the earth is to be replenished. All one has to do is go back to the very beginning, *the book of Genesis*, beginning with the first man and woman. The Bible teaches that Adam knew Eve, and she conceived and Cain was born.

In Genesis chapter, four verse one, Eve acknowledges that Cain was a gift from God; for that reason relinquishing any sovereign ownership over her own body; therefore from that moment she was subordinate to God's will regarding bringing new life into the world.

Eve recognized God as the Supreme Creator the giver of life, and that she did not have the right to take Cain's life. This did not alter her feelings, or change her role as a loving mother to Cain. I believe that she embraced motherhood as God intended.

We covered a lot of material in a few pages, and were only able to touch upon the surface concerning this great tragedy of our society. I believe that you will agree, America must be willing to reverse its decision on abortion and return to a better day to avoid punishment.

As a human race, we are the only creatures that have a living soul. This soul will never die and will live throughout eternity. It will reside in one of two places, "Heaven or Hell."

The Final Word

Who has the final word? It is not science! It is not the politician! It is God! The Bible is very clear on this subject, and you have His Word on it. *God is not a man, that He should lie, nor a son of man, that He should repent* (Numbers 23: 19a).

If you or someone you know is contemplating on having an abortion, share this message with them for consideration before they make a terrible mistake. You may save a life and a soul.

CHAPTER 5

Judgment

God Has the Final Word

Judgment Without prejudice:
> *He is the Rock, His work is perfect; For all His ways are justice, A God of truth and without injustice; Righteous and upright is He* (Deuteronomy 32: 4). *And as it is appointed for men to die once, but after this the judgment* (Hebrews 9: 27).

In Deuteronomy Moses defines God as being righteous, upright, a God of truth, perfect without injustice, and solid as a rock. There is no one whom we can compare. Moreover, in Hebrews, the writer declares we have an appointment with death and judgment.

We, are all judgment bound like it or not, we have no choice in the matter. Judgment is a topic that most people like to avoid even among the Christian community.

Because of this, I wish to devote this chapter to examine God's Word involving His role as judge. Of all the chapters, this is the most difficult because of the subject matter. The reality of judgment can be, corroborated in Scripture by two apparent truths as it applies to humankind.

First, there is judgment against the individual as seen in the life of Adam and Eve. Secondly, there is judgment against the multitude as witnessed in the great flood recorded in Genesis 6: - 8.

For all intent and purpose to maintain equilibrium between the two judgments we will take into account God's involvement with Israel and surrounding nations to discern how God interacted with them.

We will explore how God dealt with Israel and at the same time keeping in mind these boundaries involving one's conduct applying these truths to our nation and individuals as well.

A nation truly blessed by God cannot escape its moral responsibility *For everyone to whom much is given, from him much will be required; and to whom much has been committed, of him they will ask the more* (Luke 12: 48b).

Penalty for Wrongdoing

When we compare Israel, a recipient of God's blessings and punishment for wrongdoing compared to our standard of living against the rest of the world. America has surpassed all previous civilizations acclaimed by our standard-of-living measured by our industrial technology, our medical interventions, our military might, and space program to mention a few.

To establish the background material for the main topic, judgment for wrongdoing; this chapter will develop a firm foundation for God bringing punishment upon our land according to His Word. Nations and individuals alike are, judged by "what they become," not by "who they are."

There have, been a lot of speculation regarding man's dilemma viewed by what is happening in our nation. The news media carries reports of faultfinding, with little done to address the real reason that has brought this chastisement upon our land. I will make clear several truths that are vital to our understanding of this reality. These facts will enable the reader to draw their own conclusions.

When we think of punishment, assuming justice served, what comes to mind? Do thoughts like someone's misfortune, an unfair decision, a person falsely accused, wrongful facts presented, or a just penalty to be paid?

Judgment is not an easy subject matter to put in writing because none of us wishes to think that we have done anything worthy of an accusation against us that involves chastisement. To become, reacquainted, with the meaning of justice we need to review our own legal system to refresh what the fundamentals mean.

Let us look at some basic terms that describes' our modern day system of rule compared to a Theocratic {singularly ruled by God} type of government. These terms are not all-inclusive and to some extent general in nature.

The expression *judiciary* represents a structure of the law as in court system concerned with dispensing justice. The word *judge* literally means to form an opinion or one who decides. The term *judgment* stands for a decision reached and rendered by the court.

As in any institution, there is always the risk of corruption, and our system is not exempt from the temptation to be prejudiced or dishonest.

Is Justice Blind?

Fair question, unlike God's impartiality, there appears to be a double standard that exists in the way wrongdoers in many cases handled. If you are of importance or influence, such as *sports, entertainment,* member of the *elite society, business executive,* and *particularly political,* you receive different treatment.

Without providing a list many of these, you are familiar. Example in 1994, the State of California vs. Orenthal James Simpson, tried on two counts of murder. Simpson hired a high-profile defense team securing his acquittal. This believed to be one of the most publicized criminal trials in American history.

Another case of great magnitude witnessed during former President Clinton presidency when facing impeachment charges on two accusations, one of perjury and one of obstruction of justice, Despite his impeachment in 1998 by the House of Representatives later acquitted by the Senate.

The outcome of both makes noticeable a system can, and often becomes flawed because of public opinion, wealth, political pressure, lobbyist, and outside interest groups. The question remains was justice served in either case.

What struck me during the whole impeachment process including the alleged sexual misconduct accusations and broken trust with the American people, the polls continued to show overwhelming support by the people. During that time, one particular fixation that stood head-and-shoulders above the rest revealed that economics were more important than one's, morals.

It became obvious that moral behavior in the country was not as important. Many believe that, moral values are outdated and are no longer relevant in the twenty-first century. As long as humanity functions without moral leadership this becomes the norm, and we the minority lack the moral courage or strength to buck-the-system.

When moral standards no longer recognized as valuable to one's society it spills over into other professions. This is one reason why our judicial system is tainted. Many of those appointed or elected into these positions long ago quit seeking divine guidance in the decisions they make, and are ethically bankrupt themselves.

The Statue of Justice is supposed to be blind and fair as illustrated by the blindfold and balanced scales. It is becoming increasingly difficult for those in positions of authority to administer impartial justice to those whom have broken the law. For that reason, many decisions handed down are self-serving to avoid finger pointing. It has become much easier to endure public ridicule than to do what is right.

Some today as in Ezekiel's time wish to associate this kind of behavior with God, implying God is partial and unjust Ezekiel 18. Nothing can be further from the truth; God assures them that He is impartial because all souls are His. Unlike man who has limitations, God's cannot nor can He be tempted or bribed. Unlike man, His judgment is just and without fault.

There are certain attributes that belongs to God that man will never possess. God is omnipresence meaning all present; omnipotent meaning all powerful, and omniscience meaning all knowing. All that God needs He already has. All that man needs God must provide, as we will see.

A Model Nation Born

When God called Abraham to leave his home and go into a strange land. This began the birth of the Hebrew nation. What is interesting God took the initiative and called Abraham, not the other way around? This is important in understanding God's love and mercy toward humankind.

This new society would serve as the model to enlighten the world concerning the coming of Jesus Christ to know the fullness of God and His plan of redemption. It was through His chosen people that God would bless the world.

Israel and the rest of the world would soon learn of His righteous requirements for holy living. They would learn of His punishment against those who rebel according to His Word.

Everything that applied to this new nation from inception until present day applies to us today. God does not have a double standard as some men do.

From Abraham to Israel's exodus from Egypt it is important to note that God spoke through the Patriarchs such as Abraham, Isaac, and Jacob. Their duties were priestly in nature, and they were responsible for the spiritual welfare of their people.

In simple terms, God made His presence known through His spokespersons. One cannot discount historical evidence and remain true to self. God continues to speak today through His written word and His anointed if we will listen.

From Theocracy to Monocracy

The single event signifying God as ruler was the giving of the law to Moses on Mount Sinai. God ruled through Moses, then Joshua, and Judges like Samuel the last judge appointed by God.

From the time of Israel's deliverance by Moses from their bondage in Egypt, until the time of Samuel, Israel was ruled as a Theocracy meaning "God Himself is ruler." During Samuel's reign, the people of Israel wanted a king to judge them like their neighbors.

Their complaint was that Samuel was getting old. Naturally, Samuel thought they had rejected him, God knowing their true motive was about to set the record straight when He instructed Samuel to, *"Heed the voice of the people in all they say to you; for they have not rejected you, but they have rejected Me, that I should not reign over them"* (1 Samuel 8: 7).

When a society or individual no longer wants God to have a part in their lives similar to Israel rejecting God as ruler anything can happen. The depth of a nation's moral decay can only be, measured, by the depth of one's rejection of God.

A prime example relating to this instance God commanding Samuel to forewarn the children of Israel what was going to happen because of rejecting Him. When a nation rejects God opens the door for all kinds of evil to flourish.

There is solid evidence of our nation's moral decline foreseen in taking prayer out of schools and stopping Bible reading; removing the Ten Commandments in public places; forbidding people to pray in the name of Jesus in public gatherings; passing laws sanctioning abortion, allowing pornography to flourish, permitting same sex marriages to mention a few.

When these things occur, we can anticipate that terrible things will happen as God promised it would.

> *So Samuel told all the words of the Lord to the people who asked him for a king.' And he said, "this will be the behavior of the king who will reign over you: He will take your sons, and appoint them for his own chariots and to be horsemen, and some will run before his chariots. He will appoint him captains over his thousands and captains over his fifties, will set some to plow his ground and reap his harvest, and some to make his weapons of war and equipment for his chariots. He will take your daughters to be perfumers, cooks, and bakers. And he will take the best of your fields, your vineyards, and your olive groves, and give them to his servants. He will take a tenth of your grain and your vintage, and give to his officers and servants. And he will take your male servants, your female servants, your finest young men, and your donkeys, and put them to his work. He will take a tenth of your sheep, and you will be his servants. And you will cry out in that*

day because of your king whom you have chosen for yourselves, and the Lord will not hear you in that day." Nevertheless the people refused to obey the voice of Samuel; and they said, "No, but we will have a king over us, that we also may be like all the nations, and that our king may judge us and go out before us and fight our battles" (1 Samuel 8: 10 – 20).

One should not, be misled to think because God allowed Israel to have a king that He relinquished His rule or would withhold His judgment from them. Samuel was educating them on what would happen because Israel no longer wanted God as their ruler. Warning them, a king or oppressor would compel the people without mercy according to the manner of the rulers around them.

The surrounding tyrants forced their people to be servants to them and became lord and master over them. Is not our own government causing its people to become slaves to their rules?

We are fast becoming a socialist nation, soon to be controlled by a tyrannical form of government. We no longer have true representation in our government, and the people's voice goes unheard. The party agenda becomes more important over what the people might want. We become pawns in a political machine.

The government will take from you and give to another meanwhile others get rich as described in the Scripture above. We are already seeing evidence of this happening. God is not limited to what kind of punishment He will bring upon a nation.

God's Impartial Judgment

Humankind in spite of their achievements involving, science, education, economics, inventions, or social status will always demonstrate partiality in this life. God is impartial! He is the same yesterday, today, and tomorrow which is crucial. The nations surrounding Israel were well aware of God's laws and His rule over Israel.

Just as surely as God would judge Israel for wrongdoing, any nation living contrary to these laws, would bring God's impartial wrath upon them. This truth confirmed in the destruction of Nineveh and Sodom and Gomorrah. Let us examine the destruction of Nineveh and see how this truth applies.

In the Old Testament we have the story of that great city Nineveh founded by Nimrod, Noah's great-grandson. In the book of Nahum, particular chapter three, the prophet denounces a woe against Nineveh whom God was going to bring final judgment because of their wickedness. *Your injury has no healing, your wound is severe. All who hear news of you will clap their hands over you, for upon whom has not your wickedness passed continually* (Nahum 3: 19)?

In essence, they were beyond the hope of no return because of their wickedness. Because of their oppression, the nations around them will clap for joy. Is not America being laughed at today?

What is interesting earlier Jonah commanded by God to go to Nineveh to warn against pending judgment because of their sins caused the people of Nineveh to repent under Jonah's preaching? That great city repented at his warning, and God gave Nineveh a reprieve for two hundred fifty years.

Apparently, memories faded, God soon forgotten, and Nineveh sunk back into the mire of sin. True to His Word, in 612 B.C., Babylon destroyed the city without a trace as prophesied by the prophet Nahum.

Worthy of note, Nineveh best known for her arrogance, treachery, violence, faithlessness, their pride, and arrogance blinded them from the truth of their immoral condition sealing their destruction. Does this sound to familiar, do we see any similarities' to America?

I believe there are many similarities we can draw between Nineveh and America. Has not our pride, arrogance, violence, and faithlessness blinded us to the same truth denying our immoral condition.

Christian polls indicate that we are becoming more, faithless about what we believe about the Bible as time passes. Can, we as a nation turn back the clock of judgment, or have we like Nineveh gone too far?

Before we dismiss this as an ancient story without any possible connection to us today, listen what Jesus had to say on the matter. *The men of Nineveh will rise up in judgment with this generation and condemn it, because they repented at the preaching of Jonah; and indeed a greater than Jonah is here* (Matthew 12: 41).

Nineveh repented at Jonah's warning of God's judgment causing a whole nation to repent. What judgment can America expect when we have Christ's word and ignore its truth?

This edict of accountability ordained by God should not come as a surprise to us. Jesus not only confirms the story but also uses it as a warning to all who follow in their path. We hold our citizens in account for wrong deeds done against our society based upon our laws. Yet we want to deny God the same privilege or right to act accordingly.

If we continue to be unrepentant, or unremorseful after all of God's blessings through Christ has bestowed upon us. What judgment may we not expect?

Obedience and Disobedience

There are two basic principles that govern blessings or punishment that involves obedience and disobedience. Each in direct proportion to the deeds involved at the time. To understand God's punishment one must first look at the promises made to those who obey.

In the books of Leviticus and Deuteronomy, Moses warns the people of Israel what destruction God will bring upon them if they fail to obey His Commandments. Leviticus is unique in that it is broken down into two parts according to the understanding of the original Hebrew text.

The first part deals with the law and the priestly character of Israel. The second part deals with holiness and sanctification of human life. This involves terms of daily living relating to the nation of

Israel's welfare. The picture Moses describes is challenging to keep, but not without guarantee to say the least.

> *If you walk in My statues, and keep my commandments, and perform them, then I will give you rain in its season, the land shall yield its produce, and the trees of the field shall yield their fruit. Your threshing shall last till the time of vintage, and the vintage shall last till the time of sowing; you shall eat your bread to the full, and dwell in your land safely. I will give peace in the land, and you shall lie down, and none will make you afraid; I will rid the land of evil beast, and the sword will not go through your land. You will chase your enemies, and they shall fall by the sword before you. Five of you shall chase a hundred, and a hundred of you shall put ten thousand to flight; your enemy shall fall by the sword before you. For, I will look on you favorably and make you fruitful, multiply you, and confirm My covenant with you* (Leviticus 26: 3 – 9). *The Lord will open to you His good treasure, the heavens, to give the rain to your land in its season, and to bless all the work of your hand. You shall lend to many nations, but you shall not borrow. And the Lord will make you the head and not the tail; you shall be above only, and not be beneath, if you heed the commandments of the Lord your God, which I command you today, and are careful to observe them* (Deuteronomy 28: 12 – 13).

The promises made to Israel, both blessings and punishment though wide-ranging in nature, contained unalterable truths. The blessings of God were abundant and inexhaustible. These "promises" ensured their physical and economic wellbeing as well as their security provided they would walk in God's statues.

Only a powerful loving God could make and keep such promises. Those same measures would apply to punishment causing just the opposite.

The significance of all this best understood according to Jewish teachings. The promise of rain for example, was of extreme importance because in the Holy Land without it would result in famine.

The promise of peace in the land would be without value unless enjoyed in tranquil harmony without the fear of war or some dreaded disease.

The promise, the sword will never fall upon Israel by an enemy army, ensures them against invasion. The numbers put to flight expressed in round figures, showing that Israel will always be able to overcome any odds with God's help. What more could Israel ask for?

There was a time when America experienced the same confidence and security within and outside its borders. These promises intended for the masses equally apply to the individual's well-being by obeying God.

If Israel's obedience guarantees God's favor and blessings, as a reminder, their disobedience must invoke His punishment. Because of its severity the wages for disobedience portrayed by Jewish Scholars is in more elaborate details than the blessings were, especially pertaining to the punishments that would occur upon a disobedient people.

Look what God has to say about what will happen if Israel does not keep His Statues and Commandments.

> *But if you do not obey Me, and do not observe all these commandments; and if you despise My statues, or if your soul abhors My judgments, so that you do not perform all My commandments, but break My covenant, I also will do this to you: I will even appoint terror over you, wasting disease and fever which shall consume the eyes and cause sorrow of heart. And you shall sow your seed in vain, for your enemies shall eat it. I will set My face against you, and you shall be defeated by your enemies. Those*

who hate you shall reign over you, and you shall flee when no one pursues you. And after all this, if you do not obey Me, then I will punish you seven times more for your sins. I will break the pride of your power; I will make your heaven like iron and your earth like bronze. And your strength shall be spent in vain; for your land shall not yield its produce, nor shall the trees of the land yield their fruit (Leviticus 26: 14 – 20). *The alien who is among you shall rise higher and higher above you, and you shall come down lower and lower. He shall lend to you, but you shall not lend to him; he shall be the head, and you shall be the tail. Moreover all these curses shall come upon you and pursue and overtake you, until you are destroyed, because you did not obey the voice of the Lord your God, to keep His commandments and His statues which He commanded you* (Deuteronomy 28: 43 – 45).

These prophetical warnings categorized in an intentional order and measured by their increased intensity in direct proportion to Israel's resistance to obey God. Here we see God's punishment meted out based upon the severity of rebellion.

In other words, the punishment fits the crime. They are, categorized by the sickness of the people, fear throughout their land, a lack of prosperity, and even to their exile to another country.

In other words, God exacts whatever measure it takes to turn a disobedient people back to Him in order to save their soul from an eternal hell. His punishment never judged as cruel but perceived as love of a parent correcting a wayward, child.

The intention is to humble the Israelites, and cause them to realize how weak they are without God's blessings. The diseases or illnesses mentioned will strike terror especially to those persons whom become afflicted. The expression *I will set my face against you* will cause the children of Israel to become unnerved even if the threat is not real. They will continually live in fear of an enemy attack.

Are we not experiencing some of this today? A good example of our fear was the "Air Force One" photo shoot over New York City. We live in fear of an attack from rogue nations such as North Korea, or Iran.

The words *seven times more* confirm the increased intensity of God's punishment that will occur, if they do not obey Him. Their arrogance or vanity is the results of their pride, reflected in their self-reliance and prosperity. All this will be, taken from them as indicated by the illustration *heaven like iron, and your earth like bronze.* The clear indication here is the heavens will not produce rain or the earth its fruit.

I believe the children of Israel knew fully the, "what for and why to," regarding the promise of both blessing and cursing. God's withdrawal of His blessings from Israel should never be interpreted evil. Because of His holiness, God abhors evil, and nothing unholy or sinful will inherit eternal life in heaven.

It is His love to correct and protect them as any father would his child from a devil's hell. I believe that without any formal announcement by the prophet they knew, blessed or cursed, what was going on around them. Are we as wise in America?

Examining the Evidence

If Israel was aware of God's divine wrath for wrong doing, should we not be as wise giving what is happening in America. The intelligent person today using deductive reasoning should easily recognize both blessing and cursing as forewarned in the Scripture. The violence from within and the threat of destruction from without supports the evidence that we are being, judged.

When I wrote this, what happened on September 11, 2001, had not occurred. Since then, we find ourselves as a nation at war again with no certainty of the outcome. If you have been keeping up with the news, the outcome does not look too bright. Some news sources attribute the war in Afghanistan is now the longest war in American history with no real win in sight.

As the above Scriptures imply with conviction, if there is no peace in the land and you are afraid to go to bed at night then you are not being, blessed! We are a nation locked in fear, and in desperate need of divine help.

For the first time in our history, our borders are no longer safe and secure. In fact, we have reached a point we no longer have control over our own borders, or those who invade our land.

What about the diseases, and sicknesses that are plaguing our land today, many of them are without cure. All one has to do is read the headlines, or watch the news on their local newscast to see what is being reported. There is rarely a day that goes by without the news of a murder, a rape, a robbery, or the threat of being attacked.

Another truth we cannot escape nor deny that coincides with Scripture, denouncing our nation as a world power and leader? If we think, we continue to hold the same influence in the world today held at the end of the Second World War we are only kidding ourselves.

To continue the appearance as a world leader we have been, reduced to buying favoritisms from our neighboring nations. Our leaders have lost respect both at home and abroad.

Almost without exception, every military or peacekeeping effort our country has engaged in for nearly five decades has failed in some major aspect. All spent in vain, as God said would happen. My prediction is that it will get worse.

To add to the list of woes God said would happen which cannot be ignored, addresses the economic condition of our country. We have without doubt, become the largest debtor nation in the world, and are no longer the head but the tail. We are a people that have abandoned its financial responsibility in both the private and business sector.

I believe as a general population we are racing toward an economic meltdown facing trillions of dollars in debt. Giving current spending it is, estimated that by 2015 we will be almost 20 trillion dollars in debt. A debt no nation can sustain.

If by now you have reached the same conclusion I did, then the next sentence will not come as a shock. There are implications everywhere that God has set His face against us as Moses said would happen. This should not come as a great surprise. God through His love has tried to warn America by making known His intentions as He did to Abraham concerning the destruction of Sodom and Gomorrah. *And the Lord said, "shall I hide from Abraham what I am doing"* (Genesis 18: 17).

God does not bring judgment without first warning. His ministers have been forewarning our nation for some time now that God would punish our land for our wrong deeds. Despite these warnings our nation continued to ignore it, there advice was not, taken very seriously, life as usual continued to be the norm rather than heed the warnings.

More Bad News

The bad news is that God will continue to set His face against us, and His punishment will intensify as long as we continue to disobey Him. Why, because God's holiness demands it, He must be true to His Word.

Examples of this are the increase of catastrophic events that have taken place involving oil spills, earthquakes, floods, fires, tornadoes, and hurricanes. Case in point the hurricanes spanning a period of nearly a decade, between 2004 and 2012, are Charlie, Katrina, Sandy, Ike, Wilma, and Ivan, Irene, Rita and Frances costing billions dollars claiming a number lives.

These external events do not imply that all of God's ways to punish will happen simultaneous. Only God knows the outcome that will be, felt, for years to come. It simply means that God will exact whatever punishment, whether external or internal, necessary to bring about a moral change in our land.

As I am writing this, I am watching the news about our nation's election results for election 2000. Political walls now erected where only the party matters, and domestic problems put on hold to the determent of our land.

We have been, reduced to cheating or creating the appearance of cheating in order to win. The fallout from all this confusion will not be, known for several years to come. The internal damage that is being, done is insuperable.

All the polls; the spin misters; the biased news media; the referred to hired guns; the riot mongers, all clearly indicate that we are a divided nation. This was undeniably obvious during the 2008 and 2012 elections and recent Healthcare debate when both parties could not agree and divided along party lines.

Vote after vote, regardless of "Bill" was, primarily split down party lines with few exceptions. The Bible incontestably teaches that a divided kingdom or house cannot stand when pitted against itself. *If a kingdom is divided against itself, that kingdom cannot stand. And if a house is divided against itself, that house cannot stand* (Mark 3: 24 – 25).

A Voice from The Past

There was another time in our nation's history when we were a divided and a confused people. Abraham Lincoln addressed this to our nation, in his "Thanksgiving Day Proclamation." This bears repeating; much can be, learned from it!

"THANKSGIVING DAY PROCLAMATION"

"It is the duty of nations as well as of men to own their dependence upon the overruling power of God, to confess their sins and transgressions in humble sorrow, yet with assured hope that genuine repentance will lead to mercy and pardon, and to recognize the sublime truth announced in the Holy Scriptures and proven by all history, that those nations only are blessed whose God is the Lord.

We know that by His divine law, nations like individuals are subjected to punishments and chastisements in this world. May we not justly fear that awful calamity of civil war which now desolates the land may be a punishment inflicted upon us for our presumptuous sins, to the needful end of our national reformation as a whole people? But we have forgotten God. We have forgotten the gracious hand which preserved us in peace and multiplied and enriched and strengthened us, and we vainly imagined, in the deceitfulness of our hearts, that all those blessings were produced by some superior wisdom and virtue of our own. Intoxicated with unbroken success, we have become too self-sufficient to feel the necessity of redeeming and preserving grace, too proud to pray to the God who made us.

It has seemed to me fit and proper that God should be solemnly, reverently, and gratefully acknowledged, as with one heart and voice, by the whole American people. I do therefore invite my fellow citizens in every part of the United States, and also those who are at sea and those who are sojourning in foreign lands, to set apart and observe the last Thursday of November as a day of Thanksgiving and praise to our magnificent Father who dwelleth in the heavens."

I ask that you take note of the second paragraph depicting a nation gone wrong. This could just as easily been written for what we have become today. We have forgotten the gracious hand, which preserved us in peace.

No one could have said it better. We vainly imagine in the deceitfulness of our hearts that all those blessings were, produced, by superior wisdom and virtue of our own.

Intoxicated with success, we have become too self-sufficient to feel the necessity of redeeming and preserving grace, too proud to pray to the God who made us.

Whose Responsibility Is It?

Leadership plays a paramount role regarding moral influence in any society both good and bad; therefore, we all are responsible. The Bible is very clear on this subject. Those who rule and pass laws are to rule according to God's moral law and not their own interest.

National laws are intended to be compatible with God's laws the schoolmaster to bring us to Christ. For that reason, chaste laws prick our conscience when we break them, reminding us of our broken relationship with our Creator.

In Paul's letter to the church in Rome, he solemnly declares the mind of God upon the subject.

> *Let every soul be subject to the governing authorities. For there is no authority except from God, and the authorities that exist are appointed by God Therefore whoever resists the authority resists the ordinance of God, and those who resist will bring judgment on themselves. For rulers are not a terror to good works, but to evil. Do you want to be unafraid of the authority? Do what is good, and you will have praise from the same. For he is God's minister to you for good. But if you do evil, be afraid; for he does not bear the sword in vain; for he is God's minister, an avenger to execute wrath on him who practices evil. Therefore you must be subject, not only because of wrath but also for conscience sake. For because of this you also pay taxes, for they are God's ministers attending continually to this very thing. Render therefore to all their due: taxes to whom taxes are due, customs to whom customs, fear to whom fear, honor to whom honor* (Romans 13: 1 – 7).

The statement *authorities exist are appointed by God* refers to civil authorities, and literally means that if they are appointed by God, they are accountable to God. Those appointed or elected leaders, regardless of what level of service who resists God's moral law, will not be exempt from judgment based upon the choices they make or the laws they pass.

The phrase *Therefore whoever resists the authority resists the ordinance of God, and those who resist will bring judgment on themselves* contains a double-edged promise. It is, primarily intended for anyone who sets himself or herself against the moral order of God or refuses to obey those who are Godly appointed over them.

For this to work we have to make the assumption, that the ruler is a good man, as the law supposes him to be depicted in the Scripture. The Apostle explains that rulers should be role models to the people responsible to them.

He reminds the people they are to be subject unto the higher powers; and that rulers are not a terror to good works rather to give praise to those subject to their rule. Moreover, the powers entrusted to them are not for terror and oppression of the upright but to punish the wicked.

Rulers are to be in harmony with God's moral laws, not subversive to them as we are seeing today. They cannot serve two masters. *No one can serve two masters; for either he will hate the one and love the other, or else he will be loyal to the one and despise the other. You cannot serve God and mammon* (Matthew 6: 24).

Either they serve God, or they serve the world. Immoral decisions cannot be justified before God by our courts (any court) based upon some misinterpreted amendment, as we have seen recently to satisfy sinful appetites.

It is interesting to note, nowhere does Scripture require a person to follow blindly those in authority acting outside the moral order of God. Especially if imposed upon them to denounce Christ and surrender their God given convictions as the Apostle Peter taught. *But Peter and the other apostles answered and said: "We ought to obey God rather than men "*(Acts 5: 29).

Paul reminds them and us that, there is no absolute power but God's, or simply God is the origin of all power. God can delegate authority to whomever He chooses.

As with any authority comes grave responsibility, whether one sits on the highest court, or holds the highest office in the land. God will hold them accountable for their actions regardless of their station in life. The quicker our leaders learn the truth the better off we will be.

The Judas Complex

The Bible is clear in the fact that a time will come when men will no longer endure sound doctrine. People will depart from the truth and enticed away according to their evil desires. The Apostle Paul in his second letter to Timothy warns the young minister of the coming state of affairs.

> *For the time will come when they will not endure sound doctrine, but according to their own desires, because they have itching ears, they will heap up for themselves teachers; and they will turn their ears away from the truth, and be turned aside to fables* (2 Timothy 4: 3-4).

The fundamental warning is that a time will come when many in a congregation will no longer hear the biblical truths of the gospel and will seek a fairy-tale worship. This truth equally applies to a nation who neglects its moral responsibility.

We think all we have to say is "God Bless America" and all is, forgiven. I call this the Judas Iscariot complex. This concept of worship reminds me of a truth about Judas Iscariot found in (Matthew 26).

Jesus is celebrating the Passover with His disciples when He tells them that one of them will betray Him. They began to ask; *Lord is it I?* Unlike the others Judas showing disdain for Jesus asks; *Rabbi is it I?* The other disciples asked because they wanted to know if they had done something wrong and were not aware.

In their mind Jesus was still Lord because the way they addressed their question. Judas, who already knew the answer, showing lack of feeling for Jesus, uses the name "Rabbi" or teacher was asking for a different reason.

One, he was secretly hoping that the Lord really did not know it was him though Jesus had already identified the one who would betray Him. Second, Judas was fishing for a pass from the Lord. The pass never came. The Lord is not giving passes to those who know to do better and refuse to do so.

Would you be shocked to learn that across the broad spectrum of people, even among some religious persons, many do not believe it is immoral to have an abortion? To look at pornography, have sexual relations with someone of the same sex or the opposite sex in and out of wedlock. To tell a lie, as long as it is a white lie, or taking something that does not belong to you, like taking something from work, without permission.

We could never be more wrong in that assumption. The truth they are running from requires them to conform to the teachings of Christ depriving them of their sins they have come to desire and love.

Perhaps like Judas, they know the answer before they ask; "Am I doing wrong," looking for a pass that will never come without confession and repentance. To avoid sound doctrine they turn away from the truth, and seek like-minded council from their pers.

Bringing it to its Logical Conclusion

Only you can derive your own assessment concerning the current condition of our nation. May I encourage you to do your own homework. Detailed scriptural information been provided to assist you in your own study.

Explore why we have runaway debt, housing crisis, out of control health care, severe unemployment, poor economy, natural disasters, riots, unsecure boarders, and a nation divided along party lines just to mention a few.

It appears that everything tried so far has failed to recover our nation's stability and has resulted with no solution in sight.

In closing, I am reminded, the Psalmist David said, the *wicked shall be turned into hell, and all nations that forget God* (Psalms 9: 17). When you compare how we are to live, established in Part I, and how we are living today what deductions can you draw.

In conclusion, we must not forget our God is a God of love, mercy, and pardon, provided we will listen and be willing to change as pointed out. You be the judge, God Bless!

SCRIPTURE REFERENCES

Old Testament:

Genesis	[1:1] [1:26a-27] [1:28] [2:16-17, 3:1-5] [6:5-8] [6:8] [9:25] [18:17]
Exodus	[21:22-23]
Leviticus	[18:1-4, 6] [18:24-29] [26:3-9]
Numbers	[23:19a]
Deuteronomy	[6:1-9] [18: 9-12] [19:14] [27:17] [28:12-13] [28:43-45] [32:4]
Joshua	[1:-2:]
I Samuel	[8:7] [8:10-20]
Psalm	[51:5] [79:4, 8-9, 80:3-7] [80:5] [91:11-12] [139:13-14]
Proverbs	[22:28]
Isaiah	[43:10-11]
Jeremiah	[1: 4-5]
Ezekiel	[18:1-32] [18:]
Nahum	[3:19]
Zechariah	[9:9]

New Testament

Matthew	[6:24] [12:41] [13:33] [16:6]
Mark	[3:24-25]
Luke	[12:48b] [19:40] [20:20-25]
John	[1:3] [8:32]
Acts	[5:22-42] [5:29]
Romans	[1:18-28] [2:5-6] [13:1-7]
1 Corinthians	[1:18-25] [14:33]
Galatians	[6:7]
2 Timothy	[4:3-4]
Hebrews	[9:27] [10:30-31]
1 Peter	[1:17]

www.ingramcontent.com/pod-product-compliance
Lightning Source LLC
Chambersburg PA
CBHW071451040426
42444CB00008B/1285